IF WE ARE WOMEN

Joanna McClelland Glass

Playwrights Canada Press
Toronto • *Canada*

If We Are Women © Copyright 1994 Joanna McClelland Glass

Playwrights Canada Press is the publishing imprint of
the Playwrights Union of Canada (PUC): 54 Wolseley St., 2nd fl.
Toronto, Ontario CANADA M5T 1A5
Tel: (416) 703-0201 Fax: (416) 703-0059

Playwrights Canada Press operates with the generous assistance of The Canada Council - Writing and Publishing Section, and Theatre Section, and the Ontario Arts Council.

Front cover photo by Michael Cooper. Playwright photo by Jerry Bauer.
Front cover: (left to right) Pat Hamilton, Diane D'Aquila, Ruth McIntosh, Rita Howell - Canadian Stage Company, Toronto, 1994.

Canadian Cataloguing in Publication Data
Joanna McClelland Glass,
     If we are women
A play
ISBN 0-88754-532-7
I. Title.
PS8563.L3814 1994   C812'.54   C94-930886-2
PR9199.3.G5314 1994

First edition: June 1994.
Second printing: September 1994 Third printing: March 1996.
Fourth printing, January 1998.
Printed and bound in Winnipeg, Manitoba, Canada.

If We Are Women

Joanna McClelland Glass' plays have been produced across North America, and in England, Ireland, Australia and Germany. Her one-act plays, *Canadian Gothic* and *American Modern*, were first produced at the Manhattan Theatre Club in New York City, in 1972. *Artichoke*, starring Colleen Dewhurst, was first produced at Long Wharf Theatre, New Haven, Connecticut, in 1974. *To Grandmother's House We Go*, starring Eva LeGallienne, was first produced at the Alley Theatre, Houston, Texas, moving to Broadway in 1980. *Play Memory*, directed by Harold Prince, premiered at the McCarter Theatre, Princeton, N.J., and moved to Broadway in 1984, garnering a Tony nomination. *Yesteryear* was produced by the Canadian Stage Company, Toronto, in 1989. *If We Are Women* premiered in the U.S. in the summer of 1993 at the Williamston Theatre Festival, Williamston, Mass. The 1994 Canadian premiere was a co-production between The Vancouver Playhouse, and the Canadian Stage Company.

In 1984-85, Joanna Glass was awarded a Rockefeller grant enabling her to take the position of playwright-in-residence at Yale Repertory Theatre, writing a work-in-progress, *Towering Babble*. Other grants include the National Endowment for the Arts - 1980, and the Guggenheim Fellowship - 1981.

Ms Glass has written two novels, "Reflections on a Mountain Summer", published by Alfred A. Knopf in 1975, and "Woman Wanted", published by St. Martin Press in 1984. She has adapted both novels into screenplays for Lorimar Studios, and Warner Brothers.

Ms Glass was born in Saskatoon, Saskatchewan, lived and worked for 30 years in the United States, and has resided in Toronto since 1989.

For Lucy Kroll, my surrogate mother.

Production History

The American premiere of *If We Are Women* was at the Williamstown Theatre Festival, Peter Hunt - Artistic Director, Williamston, Mass., July, 1993, with the following cast:

RUTH .... *Isa Thomas*
RACHEL ....*Joanna Merlin*
JESSICA ....*Blythe Danner*
POLLY ....*Nile Lanning*

Directed by Austin Pendleton.
Set design by C. David Russell.
Lighting by Betsy Finston.
Costumes by Maureen Schell
Stage Manager - Glenn S. Crihfield Jr.
Sound by Matthew Bennett.

The Canadian premiere of *If We Are Women* was a co-production of The Vancouver Playhouse, Susan Cox - Artistic Director, and the Canadian Stage Company, Bob Baker - Artistic Director, Toronto, through January, February, and March 1994, with the following cast:

RUTH ....*Patricia Hamilton*
RACHEL ....*Rita Howell*
JESSICA ....*Diane D'Aquila*
POLLY ....*Ruth McIntosh*

Directed by Susan Cox.
Set design by Mary Kerr.
Lighting design by Kevin Lamotte.
Sound by Greg Ruddell.
Stage Manager - Rick Rinder.

The Characters

RUTH MACMILLAN *is the mother of JESSICA MACMILLAN COHEN. She is an illiterate woman in her late sixties. Her inability to read and write causes her great pain. She is visiting Connecticut from the Canadian prairies. She is, as RACHEL states in the play, "without guile": immediately likeable, open and unguarded.*

RACHEL COHEN *is the American ex-mother-in-law of JESSICA COHEN. She is a well-educated woman in her late sixties. Her energy is fired by a relentless frustration with the world, and human behavior. She's sharp, witty, stern and acerbic — a woman who has had, all of her life, one foot in intellectual endeavour and one in the kitchen.*

NOTE: Both RUTH and RACHEL were pretty when young. They should be, ideally, plump and grey-haired. (It is important that neither woman have dyed hair.) RUTH has, through the years, paid more attention to her appearance than RACHEL. RACHEL has lived very much in books, "in her head", and there is something of the aging Bohemian about her.

JESSICA MACMILLAN COHEN *is the mother of POLLY COHEN, (and Andrew Cohen, whom we do not meet) She is a writer, prairie-born, in her early forties. She is confessional, but always in a fragile, wistful, slightly humourous way, rather than self-pitying. She is wont to express herself in a florid, at times melodramatic, manner. Her lover of eight years has died in the past week.*

POLLY COHEN *is eighteen, a vibrant personality in her final year of high school. She had plans to attend Yale at the end of this present summer.*

NOTE: Throughout the play, in monologues where characters "talk to themselves", they do this energetically and conversationally, rather than soberly and internally. It is as if they are simply confiding in the audience. In these speeches, reminiscence, repose, reflection, must be avoided, or the play will "sit down" and lose momentum.

The Set and Time

The set is the back deck and kitchen of a year-round, winterized, two-story beach house near Mulberry Point, Guilford, Connecticut. The house is not isolated; it is part of a shoreline community. The nearest houses would be approximately fifty feet away on either side.

The house itself was built in the late eighteen-hundreds. It is white clapboard with dark green shutters at the windows. There must be, if not a "built" second floor, an indication of one. POLLY's bedroom is on the second floor, as are all the other bedrooms. The deck overlooks boulders, a small beach and salt marshes, directly on the shore of Long Island Sound.

An artist and a writer have lived in this house. The feeling should be more "bohemian", than modern or trendy. The furniture is worn and slightly battered white wicker with faded cushions. There is one round metal table, another wicker table, a small plastic table, a few outdoor chairs and a wicker love seat or possibly a swing. Roses might climb over an arbor, and on the deck there could be geraniums and begonias in hanging pots.

The kitchen, with appliances, should be designed as part of the whole so that action can move freely from kitchen to deck. Possibly there can be an abstract design, with a kitchen "island" behind which the actors prepare food, and behind that, the actual "wall" of cupboards and counters. There may be one, or two, entrances to the kitchen. Alongside the kitchen is a dining area. That table is set in Act Two, Scene Two. This offers interesting possibilities in the acting and direction of the "litany" on page 99.

The night before the morning of the play, after several days of hot, muggy weather, there has been a storm. The furniture has been covered with large, tarp-like cloths. These coverings should be painted to look like canvas, but could be pliable bedsheets, so that they make no noise when folded.

The other "entrance" to the deck is from a beach path, down left. This path is used by POLLY and JESSICA. There may be stairs leading from the path, up to the deck.

It is a brilliantly sunny Saturday in late June, nine a.m. The storm has left leaf and twig debris on the deck.

Act One, Scene One

*RUTH MACMILLAN faces the
audience, standing at a kitchen counter.
She is bobbing a teabag in a heavy,
unsightly, ceramic mug.*

RUTH
(*very annoyed*) I don't like the way they make tea
here. Cup by cup, with bags. Never a pot, even
when visitors come. And even when visitors
come they don't use proper teacups. (*moving
down to the deck*) Jessie's got a dozen nice, bone
china cups I sent her from Canada in the
cupboard. Never uses 'em. They call these mugs.
They're cups for lumberjacks. (*as we see
RACHEL, getting coffee in the kitchen*)
Somebody told me once that, over in India, they
save the crap to put into tea bags. Broken stems
and chips of leaves. The chaff instead of the
wheat. (*tasting it*) Tastes like sawdust. (*walking
to the edge of the deck*) Well, look at it. Ocean.
Far as you can see, all the way to the edge. Look
at it! Nothin' out there but water. Whales, I
guess, in the deep of it. Singing them sounds I
heard on T.V. If you squint — (*squinting*) —
until all the blue is gone, you could easily think
it was bald, flat prairie. Except that New York
City is seventy miles away. (*folding up one of
the "tarps"*) They have trouble here, these
Americans, saying "Saskatchewan". It gets all
snarled up in their mouths. And they're educated
people. They think "Saskatchewan" is funny.
Well, so is "Connecticut". *I* think
"Connecticut's" a helluva hoot.

*The kitchen phone rings — it is a
portable phone. Both RUTH and
RACHEL think it might be a call from
POLLY*

RACHEL   *(in the kitchen)* Hello? No, I'm sorry, she can't
come to the phone. No, I'm not her daughter, I'm
Rachel Cohen, her mother-in-law. Yes, I've seen
the books but I don't think she's autographed
them yet. Well, you see, she's had a death in the
family. *(pause)* Young man, did you just say
"you hoped it wasn't serious"? For God's sake,
man, it was a *death.*

RUTH   *(folding another "tarp")* Oh, she don't mince
words with fools.

RACHEL   Sir, I will remind her. Goodbye. *(banging down
the phone)* Miscreant!

*RACHEL enters with a coffee mug, a
rag to clean the table, and the Saturday
NEW YORK TIMES. She carries her
newspaper, a notepad, other magazines,
in a canvas tote bag.*

RACHEL   Good morning.

RUTH   Good morning. Rachel, Polly didn't come home
last night.

*RACHEL wipes down the seats at the
table, and eventually, the table itself.*

RACHEL   I know. Dances at the high school generally end
at eleven.

RUTH   Why was this one called the "last blast"?

RACHEL   It's the final dance for seniors, before the prom
next week.

RUTH   Do you think she stayed with a friend?

RACHEL	No, she'd have called. I'm afraid there's something sexual afoot.
RUTH	Well, it was only a matter of time.
RACHEL	Yes, but it's a very bad time for Jessica.
RUTH	Very bad. Did you sleep well?
RACHEL	Thank God, yes! The storm broke the humidity. That oppressive damp is hell on my bursitis.
RUTH	It left a bit of muck. (*finding an outdoor broom*) Jessie up yet?
RACHEL	Her door was open a crack. I saw her going through his bureau, sorting his clothes.
RUTH	Terrible job. Handling it all. Packing it up.
RACHEL	Yes. Having to touch all the mortal remnants. And the terrible surprises. (*pausing, remembering her own experience*) Finding bits of their hair in the brush bristles.
RUTH	I had to do it for my mum and my husband.
RACHEL	So did I.

> *This is the first break with "reality".*
> *RACHEL says the following to the*
> *audience.*

RACHEL	I never know what to say to her. It's not that I can't converse on her level, certainly I can. I just feel that I condescend, in our conversations. She doesn't seem to feel it, though, so I guess it's my problem.
RUTH	(*sweeping*) I had arthur-itis once, but it went away. It pained me something awful when I did the ironing. Back in the days when we ironed everything. And starched everything. And used bluing. Well, you remember. Sheets,

RUTH   (*continued*) pillowcases, shirts, underwear, and a clean linen hankie every day for my husband. I must have ironed ten thousand hankies in my day. God saw me on his — what does Jessie call it? The machine that God watches us on?

RACHEL   His monitor.

RUTH   God saw me, on his monitor, and he said, "Well, Ruth MacMillan's had more than her fair share of trouble." So He pushed a button and took away my arthur-itis.

RACHEL   (*referring to RUTH's cup, she shares the following opinion with the audience*) She drinks tea for breakfast. Must be some leftover vestige of something British Colonial.

RUTH   We even ironed our sanitary napkins. What did you do for pads when you were young?

RACHEL   What do you mean?

RUTH   Could you go to a store and buy Kotex pads?

RACHEL   Yes. My mother did it for me, when I started. I'm not sure it was Kotex but, yes, I remember store-bought pads.

RUTH   Ah, well, you were American and you lived in a city. We were pioneers. My mum and dad come across Canada in diapers, y'know, in 1895. Jessie showed me the oldest house in Guilford the other day. 1639. I can't even imagine 1639 because my history begins in 1895. My grandfolks cut slabs out of the prairie and made a sod hut. They ate potatoes through the first fall and through the winter they ate soup made from the skins. Just before I come down here they were talking about pioneers on the T.V., and they called our lives primitive. That pleased me, no end.

RACHEL

(*astonished*) It pleased you, to be called primitive?

RUTH

It did. Because I knew we were. I sensed it. And I was the only one in the whole damn family who did. I saw 'em out tilling once, Mum and Dad with a hand-hewn plough and two big Percheron horses. An' I said to myself, poor dumb buggers, look at 'em. Four beasts of burden. (*brief pause*) I never even heard of Kotex pads 'till I left the farm and went into Saskatoon.

RACHEL

How did you manage then, on the farm?

RUTH

What we did was rip up old flour sacks. We tore 'em into strips and then we scrubbed 'em hard, on a wash board. Then we hand-stitched the edges and we ironed them. (*putting the debris into a dustpan*) What a business! Soaking the bloody rags in pails of cold water. And sometimes, with my mum and my sisters, there'd be four of us bleeding at once. No plumbing, y'know, so all the water had to be hauled from a well. And it all had to be hidden from the men. Silly, eh? I mean, without it, nobody'd ever get born. But now I see what the ladies are talking about on T.V. They're all educated ladies, of course, and I can't always follow them. But when they say we've been compromised, I follow that.

RACHEL

You watch T.V. a lot, don't you?

> *RUTH finds her crochet bag and fishes out her yarn and a needle. She proceeds to continue crocheting one of her five-inch "medallions".*

RUTH

Oh, it's grand. Especially since Cam died. I learned more in the first month I had the T.V. than I did in twenty years before it. The T.V.'s why I'm here. I have to confess to you, Rachel, I've felt bad all these years. I'm her mother but you're the one who's always come to help her. All because I was afraid of the airplane.

RUTH	(*continued*) You came when the kids were born, you came when she divorced Gerald, and you kept coming even when the artist moved in. I have to say, Rachel, I think you're made of very good stuff.
RACHEL	Thank you. But you did see the kids every summer. They thought it was a great adventure, going up to the prairie, and they always spoke fondly of you when they came back. So you shouldn't in any way feel negligent.
RUTH	I didn't say that. I said I felt bad because I was scared of the airplane. The idea was very foreign, you know? All them people, eating and peeing up in the sky. But then the T.V. took the camera right inside, and that calmed me down, and that's why I came this time.
RACHEL	I see.
RUTH	(*worriedly*) Dear me, I wonder where the lassie is?
RACHEL	Yes, it's worrisome. Best not to dwell on it. (*pausing, looking out*) Isn't it a glorious day?
RUTH	Glorious. "June is bustin' out all over." Who's that handsome young man, down there on the rocks?
RACHEL	That's Peter, her neighbor. He's a model in New York. They come up on the weekends.
RUTH	What's he picking?
RACHEL	Sea anemones. Taking them back to the city, probably, to dry.
RUTH	What did you say was out there, across the ocean?
RACHEL	Portugal.

RUTH   Ah. I guess India's over there, too.

RACHEL   Yes, it's... (*pause: she doesn't want to get into it*) It's just somewhat beyond Portugal.

RUTH   India's where tea leaves come from. I suppose, since nobody here makes real tea, there aren't any readers around.

RACHEL   Readers?

RUTH   Tea leaf readers. We used to go every Thursday, my friend Narssie and me, and have our cups read. Then we'd spend the afternoon playin' Bingo. (*as we see JESSICA in the kitchen*) And then we'd go over to the Capitol Theatre and see a movie show. They had a gismo at the Capitol that floated clouds across the ceiling. Thursday was a big day out for Narssie and me. Trouble was, if you went long enough to the same reader, she got on to you, y'know? They get sly that way and they know what you want to be told.

RACHEL   What did you want most to be told?

RUTH   (*after a moment*) That my husband — Cam — would join A.A. (*JESSICA is heard in the kitchen, closing the refrigerator door*) There's Jess.

RACHEL   You never met him, did you?

RUTH   Who?

RACHEL   Her lover. Fleming.

RUTH   No. What did I miss?

RACHEL   Well, he was, you know, a painter.

RUTH   Of pictures, not walls.

RACHEL   Landscapes. Boats, barns, and salt marsh. He was good to her. (*finding a book review*)

RUTH	Did you think he was handsome?
RACHEL	In the way of artists. (*drawn into a review*) Verging somewhat on the derelict.
RUTH	Did you think he was — (*to the audience*) Ah, well, she loves that *New York Times*. It's the one tomorrow that kills me. You need a bloody wheelbarrow to bring in that Sunday paper. I wonder how the little delivery boys cart them? Maybe they get big, strapping men to deliver down here.

> *JESSICA enters wearing shorts and an old shirt, with a box of Martin's shirts and socks which she folds and pairs. RUTH can assist her.*

JESSICA	Good morning.
RACHEL	Good morning. Sleep well?
JESSICA	Not a wink. Jesus, this is merciless. Seven days ago I found Martin slumped over his easel — I called nine-one-one and an ambulance came — I took him to Yale-New Haven Hospital and he was dead on arrival. And last night, Polly didn't come home.
RUTH	Do you think something's amok?
JESSICA	I think it's the Kendall boy.
RACHEL	Ethan?
JESSICA	Yes.
RUTH	Well, these are her barnyard years.
RACHEL	Pardon?
RUTH	Eighteen to twenty-eight. Mounting and rutting all the time.

JESSICA	(*to RACHEL*) A prairie metaphor. (*brief pause*) God, this is so inconsiderate! And *now* of all times. Now, when I have to pack his clothing and — (*faltering*)
RUTH	Jess, we come to help.
JESSICA	How can you help? It isn't something I can delegate. I have to sort through every shirt, every sweater, every suit.
RUTH	Myself, I'd be embarrassed.
JESSICA	(*impatiently*) Pardon? Embarrassed at what?
RUTH	At the way you're packing his things. The socks need darning and the collars need turning.
JESSICA	Mother, they're going to the Salvation Army.
RUTH	I don't give a fiddler's fart where they're going. The socks should be darned and the collars turned.
JESSICA	(*angrily*) Oh, for God's sake — I can't believe you're asking me to darn socks *now*!
RACHEL	Jess, you're nervous about Polly. Don't take it out on your mother.
JESSICA	I'm nervous about these. (*pulling two ticket stubs out of a pocket*) This morning I found these ticket stubs in Martin's tweed jacket. They were to a revival of *South Pacific* at the Shubert in New Haven.
RACHEL	Memories like that are painful.
JESSICA	Rachel, I didn't attend *South Pacific* with him! I lived with that man for eight years, in absolute trust. He never mentioned seeing it. Why did he go? *When* did he go? With whom did he go? There's no date on the stubs. I cannot believe that, three days after I spread his ashes at Mulberry Point, I'm confronted with these stubs,

JESSICA   (*continued*) this doubt, this sudden specter over our lives. And I can't believe that, simultaneously, my daughter chose this morning not to be there, in her bed, hugging her threadbare Snoopy.

RACHEL sighs at this outburst

RACHEL   Oi, vey. (*then proceeding reasonably*) If you think it's Ethan Kendall, perhaps we should call his home.

JESSICA   I'll wait until noon. But what do you say? "Mrs. Kendall, my daughter didn't come home last night. Did your son come home last night? Well, Mrs. Kendall, there are four motels in Guilford. You take two, I'll take two —." God, what do you say?

RACHEL   That bookstore in New Haven called.

JESSICA   What?

RACHEL   The bookstore, The Scribe. They've got your book in the window and they're waiting for autographed copies.

JESSICA   I can't.

RACHEL   You must.

JESSICA   I can't. Can not.

Pause. Changing the subject, JESSICA looks out to the water.

What a brilliant day. Crystal clear.

RUTH   All the way to Portugal.

RACHEL   (*gazing out*) Every aspect pleases and only man is vile. And we have no men so the day is promising.

JESSICA   (*on the verge of tears*) No men.

RACHEL   (*going to JESSICA's side*) Oh, God. I'm sorry —
                I didn't —

JESSICA   Three widows.

RACHEL   (*impatiently*) Now, now, now, I think we've had
                sufficient weeping. (*trying to lighten the
                moment*) Jess, last night we were sitting out here
                quietly, in our three solitudes, and I thought:
                Samuel Beckett would put us in ashcans.

                          *RACHEL smiles, JESSICA wipes a
                          tear.*

RUTH   In what?

JESSICA   Ashcans, Mum. Samuel Beckett put people in
                ashcans, on the stage.

RACHEL   Shakespeare'd have us dancing around a cauldron.

JESSICA   Terrence Rattigan would have us at separate
                tables, in a shabby seaside tearoom.

RACHEL   Ibsen would put us in corsets, in Christiania,
                yearning to be free.

                          Brief pause.

JESSICA   Who said, "Death, thou camest when I had thee
                least in mind"?

RACHEL   (*very annoyed at her memory lapse*) Uh...Um...
                Oh, God — I swear, I've got creeping
                Alzheimer's. "Death, thou camest when I had
                thee —." I can't remember. (*returning to the
                newspaper*)

RUTH   (*to JESSICA*) You know she will.

JESSICA   Yes, Mum, she will.

> *JESSICA pauses, gazing at RUTH,
> examining her. Lighting change. The
> stage darkens, highlighting only
> JESSICA and RUTH.*

JESSICA   God, she's aged. (*turning to the audience*) Her
long, thick hair, in memory, is squashed a bit
under a Hunter Green hat. When I was little, she
washed her face with milk every morning. Went
about rather slack in the belly all week, but on
Friday night, when Dad came in off the road, she
put on a girdle. And cologne from a cobalt blue
bottle. "Evening in Paris". My God, what was
the glue between those two? Five years later it
was all gone. Her good china, her Persian rug —
all to the bootlegger. And she said to me, "If you
irk him, he'll hit you." And irk him I did.

RUTH   (*to the audience*) Bobby Burns in his lap and his
bottle by his elbow, tucked in the chair beside
him. And that dumb bugger had to have his silk
mufflers, monogrammed. Ranted on about
"sartorial splendour", without a pot to pee in or a
window to throw it out of. Well. His heart was
in the highlands but his head was up his ass.

JESSICA   (*to the audience*) And his larder was bare — but
for her. She went out to cook at the Old Folks'
home. She toiled in the kitchen of the Old Folks'
home, at minimum wage. Two dollars an hour in
those days.

> *Lighting change.*

RACHEL   There's a new biography of Chekhov. Calls him
a genius. Ha!

JESSICA   I think he was.

RACHEL   Really?

JESSICA   Yes. Emphatically.

RACHEL

(*annoyed*) It's a word that's bandied about a great deal. Nothing *happens* in Chekhov.

JESSICA

Life happens in Chekhov.

RACHEL

Really, it doesn't. All that talk, that incessant prattle, all of them lolling about in remote, rural places, lamenting their lot.

RUTH

Who was the one in the paper last Wednesday — the Swede?

RACHEL

Strindberg. August Strindberg.

RUTH

Jessie, if I could read, which one would I like?

JESSICA

Well, let's see. Probably...

RACHEL

Ruth, you amaze me.

RUTH

I do?

RACHEL

You are so without guile!

RUTH doesn't know what "guile" means.

RUTH

Really?

RACHEL

(*a transition, turning out, to the audience*) But then, so is her daughter. My son, Gerald, said so when he first met her. He'd just begun his doctorate at M.I.T. He came home one weekend and he said, "Her mother's illiterate, her father's an alcoholic, she hasn't been to college, and she's from some unpronouncable place on the Canadian prairie." I said, "Gerald, it doesn't bode well."

JESSICA

Mum, Chekhov was Russian. There's something about the Russian steppes that reminds me of the prairie. I relate to it. I think you would, too. But you wouldn't like Chekhov's people, either. You'd find them lazy.

RUTH

No gumption, eh?

RACHEL	All they did was talk and consume large amounts of tea.
RUTH	Did they make it in a pot?
RACHEL	Yes, a samovar.
RUTH	It must have been good tea.
JESSICA	You wouldn't like Strindberg at all. Strindberg was a snarling brute.
RUTH	Jess, be careful. That's what everyone called your father. They said "Campbell MacMillan's a brute and a bounder." Maybe that Swede had a lot of troubles.
JESSICA	So did Chekhov. But Chekhov had compassion, and Strindberg had spleen.
RACHEL	You understand, Ruth, I don't share that opinion.
RUTH	I do. Tell me, this Strindberg fella, was he Jewish?
RACHEL	(*taking umbrage*) I beg your pardon? No, he wasn't.
RUTH	That name isn't Jewish?
RACHEL	It's Swedish. (*impatiently*) Where the hell is the crossword? Why do they insist on burying it?
JESSICA	(*to the audience*) Poor Mum's never quite made peace with my married name. Cohen. This name I've lugged about for twenty-two years. Lugged it about long after the vows were broken and the ties were severed. And yet, of all the people I've known, Mum is entirely without prejudice. It must be something she picked up on the prairie, by osmosis.

RACHEL

(*to the audience*) Is it sheer ignorance or is it a national trait? Canadians are so anxious to snoop around in your blood lines. To label you and get you filed in a little slot. It's as if they don't know how to behave until they've got you pigeonholed. (*to JESSICA*) What's a four letter word for a European evergreen?

JESSICA

Mmmm. Ilex?

RACHEL

Ah, yes. Lytton Strachey was buried under an ilex.

RUTH

(*to the audience*) Well, I shouldn't have asked. They're so touchy on the subject. Simple enough question: is so-and-so Jewish? But it's, like, I can see Rachel bracing herself, like if so-and-so *is* Jewish I'm going to run off at the mouth with slurs. I've never done that and I certainly wouldn't start now, with my two grandchildren being half-Jewish. (*brief pause*) Where did you say Andrew was this summer?

JESSICA

Sri Lanka. It's an island at the bottom of India. It's a volunteer program, to help Third World countries.

RUTH

Third world? Must be two I don't know about.

JESSICA

(*to the audience*) When I told Mum I was marrying Gerald Cohen, she thought of old Shacter, who ran the dry goods store on Avenue A in Saskatoon.

RUTH

(*to the audience*) Shacter sold pins, needles, thread, and Scottish tartans by the yard. Cam didn't like that. "Imagine", he'd say, "him, selling tartans!"

JESSICA

(*to the audience*) I'd like to call it prairie provincialism, but I can't. How tidy it would be if one could confine it to arid little cities. (*to RACHEL*) Rachel, a month ago I went to a doctor at Yale, to tend to my sinus problem.

JESSICA	(*continued*) "Cohen", he said, reading my insurance card. Then he looked at my nose. Then he took some instrument in hand and poked it up my nose. He said, "Have you ever had an operation on your nose?" "No", I said, "never." "Cohen", he repeated suspiciously. "Are you sure?" "Absolutely", I said. But I was offended. I was offended for my children. And then I was outraged. That there still occurs a "high" — yes, the druggie's term, a high. A giddy, heady rush that courses through the blood when one human being implies to another: My nose is better than yours.

> *The phone rings. RACHEL jumps up. Again, they all hope it is POLLY.*

RACHEL   I'll get it.

> *RACHEL runs to the kitchen.*

JESSICA   That had better be Miss Polly!

RACHEL   Hello?

> *RACHEL shakes her head, "no" — it isn't POLLY.*

JESSICA   (*to RUTH*) You shouldn't have asked that.

RUTH   Jessie, don't scold. Why's everybody so touchy?

RACHEL   (*in the kitchen*) Oh, yes?

JESSICA   You don't understand their history.

RUTH   You mean Hitler?

JESSICA   Before that. Pogroms, ghettos, shtetls. They're vulnerable.

RACHEL   Yes, I see. I'm very sorry.

RUTH   I *don't* understand why she braces herself that
                way. She's got two college degrees — she was a
                teacher, for Heaven's sake.

RACHEL   Just let me find a pen.

RUTH   Vulnerable's when you can't read and write. My
                God, if I'd just gotten to Grade Eight my whole
                life would have been different. You know why,
                when you were little and we went downtown, we
                always had lunch at Pinder's? Because Pinder's
                never changed the menu, and I couldn't read the
                menu, and I could put in my order at Pinder's
                without embarrassing both of us.

RACHEL   That was WHCT?

JESSICA   Oh, shit, I forgot! I had an interview today about
                the book.

RACHEL   (*on the phone*) No, I'm her mother-in-law. I'm
                terribly sorry but, you see, she's had a death in
                the family. Well, yes, it was close. It was,
                actually, her — gentleman friend. The landscape
                painter, Martin Fleming. Yes, well, I'm sure she
                had it on her calendar, but our schedules are out
                of whack. Could you possibly call her next
                week? (*as JESSICA takes note of this*) Say,
                Wednesday? She'll be back on schedule by then.

RUTH   I'm the one with a curse on my life!

RACHEL   Thank you. Goodbye.

                *RACHEL leaves the kitchen for the
                interior of the house.*

RUTH   Trembling in church, pretending I could read the
                hymnal, mouthing words, sweating like a darkie.
                She taught grade ten for twenty years — I never
                made it through grade two! I was drug out of
                school to mind all the young ones, while Mum
                and Dad tilled the land —

RUTH &
JESSICA   (*simultaneously and quietly, by rote*) — with a hand-hewn plough.

JESSICA   Mum, please, not now.

RUTH   Why not now? Because your Martin-man died?

JESSICA   *Fleming.* You know his last name very well. Yes, not now, because Martin Fleming is dead. And all I want to do is mourn. And no one will let me. (*a sigh and mood transition*) I'm sorry. Mum, what you don't see in Rachel is her subtext.

RUTH   Oh, talk English!

JESSICA   Education isn't some kind of vaccination that makes you immune from life. Rachel's accomplished, academically, but she's frustrated. She gets agitated listening to world news, state news, county news — God, she gets frazzled reading the local *Shoreline Times.*

RUTH   Why?

JESSICA   Because we don't honour our father and mother, because we kill, commit adultery, bear false witness, covet our neighbour's...

RUTH   I get it — I get it!

JESSICA   And she has a festering regret that she didn't attend the right schools.

RUTH   Are you tellin' me there are "wrong" schools?

JESSICA   And, please, while you're down here, don't say "darkie".

RUTH   What should I say?

JESSICA   African American.

RUTH	I suppose I should say "perspiring like an African American." (*brief pause*)
JESSICA	Mum, I don't have the stamina for this today. Polly's God knows where, and Martin is — absent.
RUTH	Listen, Jess, if Martin Fleming was the world's eighth wonder, why the hell didn't you marry him?
JESSICA	Once burned, twice shy.
RUTH	Rachel says he was good to you.
JESSICA	Very good. Years ago, when Gerald saw my first bits of writing, he said, "Got to watch the syntax." He talked about parsing and dangling participles. Mum, those are the nuts and bolts of sentences — they had nothing to do with what I have to say. Gerald spoke four languages, but he didn't speak mine. He got up every morning and put on his armour — against the irregular, the unsuitable, the mispronounced. Last year I bought a potter's wheel. My first effort was a bowl. It was so lopsided, I cried. Martin hugged me and said, "Sweetie, even the Parthenon is crooked." Gerald once sent a postcard from Leningrad. "Conference going well, rubbing elbows with two Nobel laureates." Martin sent a postcard from Dublin. "Loving you, on the Liffey".
RUTH	First time you've mentioned Gerald since Andrew's accident. Do you hate him?
JESSICA	No. I rarely think of him now.
RUTH	But he flew out, didn't he? He went to see Andy at the hospital?
JESSICA	I reached him at a conference in Houston. I said, "The car's totalled and Andy's in a coma." I said, "It may be fatal, Gerald, when can you come?" He said... (*faltering at this painful memory*)
RUTH	What?

JESSICA	I could hear him fumbling in his briefcase. He said, "Let me check my calendar." He came three days later.
RUTH	Well, some wouldn't have come at all.
JESSICA	(*flaring*) What is that supposed to mean? Really, sometimes you drive me crazy! Did you even *hear* me? In a coma! May be fatal! When can you come? (*almost a growl*) "Let me check my calendar."

> *RACHEL comes in, carrying a pen and seven or eight copies of JESSICA's book, "If We Are Women."*

RACHEL	That call was WHCT.
JESSICA	I forgot completely.
RACHEL	Here — sign these.
JESSICA	(*very disturbed*) I can't. Can not.
RACHEL	(*irritatedly*) Oh, please. Of course you can!
JESSICA	I can't! (*near hysteria*) What if Polly's not with Ethan? What if she's been raped and mutilated? What if she's found in pieces — segments — fragments — in a salt marsh?
RACHEL	Oi, vey! I'm at my wits' end, Jess, with your histrionics! Their window's full of 'em, they're waiting for these copies.
RUTH	What did you call this one?
JESSICA	*If We Are Women.* (*to RUTH*) It's from an English writer, Virginia Woolf. She said, "We think back through our mothers, if we are women."
RACHEL	(*handing her a pen*) Start signing.

JESSICA

Rachel, I am quite undone. I'm undone enough, in fact, that I can say plainly to you, Rachel, you *know* me. You know me very well. You know me well enough to know that I will not be back on schedule by Wednesday.

RUTH

(*a reprimand, for her tone*) Jessica, mind your mouth.

JESSICA

You *both* know me very well. Correction. You *think* you do, but no one ever knows anyone, really, do they? No one ever gets into the other one's head, the other one's space. I mean, Christ, what a presumption to think that we know anyone well!

RACHEL

What is this about?

JESSICA

(*to RACHEL*) How *can* you get on the blower and say so blithely that I'll be back on schedule next Wednesday? What gall, Rachel, what chutzpah! Proof positive.

RACHEL

Of what?

JESSICA

Of our inability to know. Martin and I had souls that ran parallel. We were matched sets, peas in a pod and sometimes, briefly in sex, we actually melded into one. But afterwards, we reverted to ourselves. "You in your small corner, and I in mine."

RUTH

I don't follow this.

JESSICA

Mum, if someone said "boulevard", my mind leapt to ours, in Saskatoon, and Dad, dead drunk on the boulevard, pissing on the peonies in broad daylight with all the stolid neighbors, all the Anglo-Saxon sturdy burghers with their Anglo-Saxon noses pushed against their windows, peering out at Dad's cascading piss. And he *was* what they called him: he was a brutal, battering son-of-a-bitch.

RUTH	(*shocked, and near tears*) Jess MacMillan!
JESSICA	When Martin heard the word "boulevard", his mind leapt to Paris. To being twenty years old and sprinting happily down the Champs Elysées with a chunk of Gruyere cheese in hand, which he'd never before tasted and which he thought, on that day, was a discovery second in magnitude only to sex. (*to RACHEL*) What we learned, Martin and I, and we learned this torturously, was that true knowledge of the other remained a phantom. We had orgies of self-revelation. We had evenings devoid of everything but the whole truth, the plain truth, the naked truth. We dredged up hurtful old feelings, painful old incidents. What Mum said, what Dad said, what the schoolyard bully in Grade Four said. But we couldn't transfer the experience. Our parallel lines couldn't intersect. You in your small corner, and I in mine.
RACHEL	(*fuming*) Jess, these declamations of yours — these damned arias, would try the patience of a saint! Are you saying that communication is beyond our grasp?
JESSICA	I am saying, Rachel, that communication is human, but knowledge is divine. I am saying that you can't possibly know me if you can get on the fucking blower and tell an absolute stranger that I'll be back on schedule next Wednesday!
RACHEL	(*a light bulb goes on*) Anonymous!
	RACHEL runs to her notepad, to write down her recollection.
JESSICA	I beg your pardon?
RACHEL	Anonymous! "Death thou camest when I had thee least in mind." It's from the medieval play, *Everyman*. Fifteenth Century. Author unknown.

JESSICA

Rachel, I will not be diverted. Oh, I know the two of you very well! You're thinking, well, she'll have her little tantrum and then she'll get on with it. Eventually her vanity will surface and she'll wash her hair and shave her legs and put on something feminine, something see-through and peek-a-boo, something chiffon, and she'll sashay out again into the world, on the prowl, dropping her spoor, leaving her scent, until a new set of gonads comes along. And then there'll be order again. Schedules. Appointments. Dates and times and places scratched on calendars. Duties, real or concocted, to be dealt with. And at the end of the year she'll refer to the calendar and find there a chronicle of her busy-ness. Hard, written evidence that she's alive. No! (*beginning to cry*) The death of this man has left me forever altered. I'm going to call WHCT and tell them exactly that. I'm going up to my study.

JESSICA moves up to the kitchen, then returns quickly.

JESSICA

How could you, Rachel? How could you?

RACHEL

What now?

JESSICA

How could you remember that Wednesday's review was Strindberg? How could you isolate that particular bit of minutia from a day in which we took Martin's ashes and threw them off the boulders at Mulberry Point? Remembering that, Rachel, about Wednesday, can only be considered callous.

RACHEL

Callous? May I remind you, please, that you are mourning Fleming, I am not.

JESSICA

Martin! His name was Martin! (*returning to the kitchen*) Oh, where the fuck is Polly? Why is she doing this to me *now*?

JESSICA leaves the kitchen for the interior of the house.

RUTH   (*after a moment*) She ain't ever been easy.

RACHEL   No.

RUTH   I need another cup of tea. (*pause*) Another fistful of sawdust in a mug. (*looking at JESSICA's books, tapping the top one*)

RUTH   I shudder to think what's in here. Ignorance is bliss.

             RUTH exits.

RACHEL   (*waiting a moment, pacing a bit, considering JESSICA's outburst, upset*) Callous. Well. She is given to hyperbole. She's often infuriating. She has a thin patina of containment, but underneath it's anarchy. I've wondered, these twenty-two years, if I even like her.

             RUTH leaves the kitchen. Lighting change. The stage darkens, highlighting RACHEL.

How odd, to be here now. To drive up, four hours from Pennsylvania, to be at her side in her hour of grief. But I came willingly, as I always have. I came after the divorce when she was alone with the children and struggling for money. I mended and patched, I made slip-covers to hide the damage of kids and cats. And after Fleming arrived, I still came. I cooked for the four of them, my daughter-in-law, my two grandchildren, and the landscape painter. I cooked the old, Jewish dishes they requested. Blintzes and borsht, latkes, kreplach, challa, hamantashen. My friends think I've kept this relationship alive for my grandchildren. They think, because I could see my son in the kids' faces, I wouldn't mind serving up latkes to the invading landscape painter. They're wrong.

RACHEL (*continued*) There's something in her life that's
forever...(*shrugging*)...magnetic. And, repellant.
Magnetic because her writing is so mysterious.
I've thought if I could locate the source, the
wellspring that propells her pen, I, too, might
write. Why can't I? I love language, I express
myself well. Perhaps I know too much. I'd read
all of Shakespeare by the time I was twenty. I've
taught the classics, I've read reams of criticism.
But when I sit down to blank paper, my pen is
paralyzed. (*an introspective pause*) Her source is
her feelings. Deeply, zealously felt feelings. Her
profession is, essentially, one of confession.
That's what's repellant. It's not my pen that's
paralyzed, it's me. I'm ill-at-ease with the
zealously felt. Gerald was, too...not surprising.
The hand that rocks the cradle. He learned at my
knee that people impaled on their feelings never
achieve maturity. And I was right. There is
something severely...arrested about Jess.

How odd to be here now, while she mourns the
man who wasn't my son.

Curtain.

Act One, Scene Two

Noon, the same day. RACHEL brings on a plate of sandwiches, from the kitchen. RUTH is crocheting.

RACHEL How long does it take you to crochet one of those medallions?

RUTH One hour. I've got fifty done. I need three hundred for a tablecloth.

RACHEL For her dining room?

RUTH Uh huh. When Jessie's gone, the kids'll have something of her on their bookshelves. That's what she'll hand down. When I'm gone, Jessie'll have three hundred hours of my life sitting on her table. That's what I'll hand down.

RACHEL Ruth, was there ever a time in Jessie's childhood when there was a harbinger ... I mean, was there ever a sign that she'd become a writer?

RUTH (*gravely*) I knew when she was twelve that her head worked different. (*dredging up this memory with difficulty*) Her dad had...hit her, and she'd peed her pants. I come into her room and sat on her bed, and I was surprised that she was dry-eyed. It was raining. "Helluva downpour", I said. She was lookin' out her bedroom window and she said, "Mum, the windowpanes are crying."

> *Brief pause. JESSICA enters the
> kitchen.*

RUTH   I knew she wouldn't stay on the prairie and learn
          shorthand and work at the Wheat Pool.

> *JESSICA enters, carrying a plastic
> pitcher of lemonade and a tray of
> glasses.*

JESSICA   Well, I called Mrs. Kendall.

RUTH   Ah?

JESSICA   Ethan was at home.

RACHEL   (*surprised*) Was he?

JESSICA   He said Polly left the dance with someone named
          Charlie Whitman. He didn't go to Guilford High.
          He's been expelled, actually, from Choate.

RACHEL   Oh, dear.

RUTH   What's Choate?

JESSICA   It's a ritzy prep school near Wallingford. John F.
          Kennedy went to Choate. I'm giving her one half
          hour, then I call the police. (*pause*) I also called
          — well, I felt like a fool. I called the Shubert.
          South Pacific was on four months ago, in
          March. I went to Notre Dame for a week in
          March, to do seminars.

RUTH   (*carefully*) Did Martin have...a secretary?

JESSICA   (*lashing out*) Artists don't have secretaries!!

RUTH   I'm sorry!

RACHEL   He probably ran into some old buddy and took
          him to the show.

JESSICA	Rachel, men take buddies to Hartford to watch the Whalers. Men take buddies to Boston to watch the Bruins. Men don't take buddies to see *South Pacific.* What do you think? Should I call the police now? *You* probably think I should have called at six a.m. What should I do?
RUTH	(*annoyed*) Oh, go revive those roses. They're wilting.
JESSICA	How do I do that? Put 'em in the fridge? (*getting the vase*)
RACHEL	No — no — make a fresh cut —
RUTH	And put them in hot water.
JESSICA	You're kidding!

JESSICA goes to the sink, where she proceeds to cut the stems.

RACHEL	(*at the crossword*) Listerine's good, too, to revive flowers.
RUTH	A spoonful of it, in houseplants, kills pests. And marigolds around your tomatoes keep the bugs away.

A moment passes.

RACHEL	Camphor kills moths.
JESSICA	Bleach kills mildew.
RUTH	Salt soothes bee stings.
JESSICA	Soda lifts wine stains.
RACHEL	Malt beer's good for fevers.
RUTH	Molasses for constipation.
RACHEL	Porridge for diarrhea.

JESSICA   Bananas for blood pressure.

RACHEL   Broccoli for shiny hair.

                   JESSICA returns with the roses.

JESSICA   A toothbrush cleans stove knobs.

RUTH   Q-tips clean carved wood.

RACHEL   Soap's good, on a burn.

JESSICA   Aloe is better. I always keep a plant over there.

RACHEL   *(a lament)* Alas, alas, these are the things we
                   know best. *(to JESSICA)* Jess, try your hand at
                   this. I've run out of steam. *(handing the
                   crossword to JESSICA)*

                   *Lighting change. The stage darkens,
                   highlighting RUTH, RACHEL and
                   JESSICA. A moment of silence as the
                   three women withdraw entirely into
                   their thoughts.*

                   *POLLY walks up from the beach to the
                   deck. She pauses there, looking at the
                   three women. She wears the skirt and
                   blouse she wore to the dance, the night
                   before.*

POLLY   God, look at them. So solemn. *(to the audience)*
                   I don't know who they are when they're like this.
                   Especially my Grammas. I've sat across from my
                   Grammas, on porches in Saskatoon,
                   Saskatchewan and Malvern, Pennsylvania. I've
                   smelled honeysuckle wafting up from both
                   frontyards, and I've felt very close to them. Then,
                   suddenly, they gaze off into space. They look
                   out, past the railing, across the yard. Not looking
                   forward — backward. What were they thinking
                   about? Horses and buggies? Five-cent ice cream

POLLY	(*continued*) cones? Cars with running boards? Hard to imagine they were virgins once. (*the following is said with an endearing archness*) As I was, yesterday.
JESSICA	What's a "Dutch product", in four?
RUTH	Tulip?
RACHEL	Edam.
JESSICA	(*writing it in*) Yeah. Edam.
POLLY	I feel like I have to go in there and scale three mountains. I feel like I should have picks and pulleys and ropes. (*a big sigh*) They're really wonderful when they're funny — but we won't see much of that today. My mother, for instance, is very fond of literary anecdotes. For example:
JESSICA	(*to the audience, carrying the crossword*) Polly, this is great. James Joyce is in Trieste, walking along, very preoccupied, struggling with great, philosophical questions. Suddenly a young man sweeps up in front of him and bows at his feet. "Please", says the young man, "may I kiss the hand that wrote 'Ulysses'?" Joyce is horrified. He says, (*with an Irish accent*) "You may not. It's done a lot of other things, too."
POLLY	And she's very partial to this comment on the making of art.
JESSICA	This is in Florence, the day that Michelangelo unveiled his "David". A group of matrons bustles up and surrounds him. They "ew" and "aw" at the beauty of the statue. Finally, one of them takes him aside. She says, "How did you extract such a miraculous piece of art from a vast chunk of marble?" Michelangelo says, (*with an Italian accent*) "Well, I'lla tell you. I carved and I cheeselled, I cheeselled and I carved. And everything that wasn't David, I threw away."

JESSICA *goes back to the crossword.*

POLLY

Gramma Cohen's humour usually requires a Yiddish accent.

RACHEL

(*to the audience*) Polly, listen to this — it's instructive. This old Jewish lady lives all alone, on the lower East Side. She has a son who's gotten very rich in the garment business — a multi-millionaire. He comes to visit every Saturday, but this particular Saturday he walks in and she doesn't recognize him. He's been to Abercrombie and Fitch. He's got a sailor's hat with an anchor in the middle of it. He's got a navy blue uniform with epaulettes at the shoulders and lots of gold fringe. He says, "Mama, today I bought a yacht." She's making gefilte fish, she doesn't pay much attention. She says, "Good, Sammy, I'm glad." He gets angry. He says, "Mama, you don't understand! I bought a yacht. Today, Mama, I am a Captain." She's very old, she's very wise, she goes to give him a hug. She says, "Sammy, by you, you are a Captain. By me you are a Captain. But by Captains, Sammy, are you a Captain?"

POLLY

Gramma Mac loves this story about a grizzly bear.

RUTH

(*to the audience*) Polly, this is a good one. There's this tavern, eh?, way the hell up in the wilderness. A bunch of lumberjacks are sitting in there, swilling down beer, when the door opens. What comes in? A great big, burly, grizzly bear! This bear walks up to the kid at the bar and he says, "I'd like a beer, please." Well, the kid's scared shitless. He runs to the boss, and he says, "Jesus, that grizzly bear just ordered a beer!" The boss says, "Tell him it'll be ten dollars." So the kid says to the bear, "It's gonna cost you ten dollars." The bear frowns for a minute and then he says "fine". The kid gives him a beer, the bear drinks the beer, nobody utters a word. Finally, when the bear starts to leave, the kid runs after

RUTH   (*continued*) him. He says, "Y'know, we don't get too many grizzly bears in here." And the bear says, "At ten bucks a beer, I guess you don't."

                RUTH laughs, POLLY chuckles. When the laughter subsides:

JESSICA   I can't get this. What's a "piglet", in five?

RACHEL   Not....*Hamlet*...

JESSICA   In five.

RUTH   Must be a shoat.

RACHEL   A what?

RUTH   A shoat is a baby pig.

RACHEL   How do you spell it?

                JESSICA shoots a look to RACHEL — she should not have asked that.

RUTH   No idea.

RACHEL   I'm sorry —

JESSICA   (*spelling it, printing it in*) S-h-o-a-t. It fits. Great.

POLLY   Well, I have to face the music. (*beginning to enter, then pausing*) The trouble is, it's their music, and I have to make my own.

                POLLY runs onto the deck.

POLLY   Mother, I can explain this very easily —

JESSICA   Where have you been? (*running to hug POLLY*)
          Oh, thank God you're all right! (*holding POLLY
          at arms' length*) Missy, now that I know you're
          not dead, I'm going to kill you! What about
          Alexander Graham Bell? What about the mere
          courtesy of a phone call?

POLLY   It wasn't possible. I'm sorry. But I can explain
          this very simply: I'm in love.

JESSICA   (*threateningly*) Missy, I have called Mrs. —

POLLY   Mom, please, let's go inside.

JESSICA   I have called Mrs. Kendall. You were not with
          Ethan last night. You were seen, by Ethan,
          leaving —

POLLY   Please, not in front of Gramma Mac and Gramma
          Cohen —

JESSICA   Leaving the dance with one Charlie Whitman, of
          unknown address, on his motorcycle. Ethan came
          on to inform me that Charlie Whitman was
          expelled from Choate last year for behavior so
          reprehensible —

POLLY   — Your word —

JESSICA   My word — so reprehensible he has since been
          refused at three universities. I want to know,
          Missy, why you were not with Ethan Kendall
          last night?

POLLY   The question is...peculiar.

JESSICA   Answer it!

POLLY   I mean, like, are you implying that if I'd been
          with Ethan all night, it would be O.K.?

JESSICA   Why this Hell's Angels, Harley-driving twerp
          rather than Ethan?

POLLY	I'll tell you why. Because Ethan Kendall's an adolescent boy, and Charles Whitman is a man. (*a beat*) A very manly man.
JESSICA	A manly man? He's barely out of knickers. You'll have to give him shaving lessons, for God's sake!
POLLY	When your sanity returns, you'll want to talk privately. You owe me an apology.
JESSICA	You expect *me* to —
POLLY	I do. Charles Whitman is not a twerp. I'm going up to my room.

> *POLLY storms off. JESSICA is near tears.*

JESSICA	Why do I feel so strange? So personally — violated?
RACHEL	(*a criticism*) Strong word, that.
RUTH	(*to JESSICA*) I did, too, years ago, when you — were.
JESSICA	I never told you.
RUTH	I knew.
JESSICA	I wasn't violated.
RACHEL	Nor was she, probably. Consenting adults, probably.
JESSICA	(*making a small moan*) Oh, Jesus! How strange!
RUTH	What's the matter?
JESSICA	One of Dad's dirty old jokes has just leapt to mind. About someone spying on two kids in a park.

> *JESSICA slowly "examines" the images in the following. She does this gravely, so as to kill the possibility of an easy laugh for the audience.*

JESSICA

"His pants were down
His ass was bare
His balls were dangling in the air
His you-know-what was you-know-where.
If that ain't fuckin'
I wasn't there."

Do you know why that little ryhme is suddenly obscene? Because I remember, first, the breath. Baby's breath. The first bath, the clink of the spoon when it hits the first tooth, the first steps. And remembering that, really quite vividly, "you-know-what — you-know-where" is a violation.

RACHEL

Bound to happen.

JESSICA

Yes, but I'd assumed with Ethan. I know where he lives. I see his dad at the bank. They'll be at Yale together this fall. And Ethan Kendall's the handsomest boy in Guilford. What should I do? *(to RACHEL, who is ready to offer advice)* Don't tell me. Let me think.

> *JESSICA heads to the beach path, and off.*

RUTH

Ah, well, handsome's in the eye of the beholder. I remember once, seeing only the back of a man. A thin, unmuscular man. When he turned around, he was homely as a mud fence. But what drew my attention, really, was the way his jacket sleeves fell on the cuffs of his shirt. I mean, it had nothing to do with tailoring. It all had to do with his wrists. There was a beauty about his hands, and I wanted that man.

RACHEL

Did you have him?

RUTH

Goodness, no. The feeling held me in its grip, though, for almost a week.

RACHEL

What feeling?

RUTH

I don't know what you call it, but I wanted those hands on my breasts.

RACHEL

(to the audience, as the stage darkens, highlighting her) What I feel, when this sort of talk rolls around, is abject horror. That if I participate, candidly, I'll be reduced to some lower level. Some other species. Something "sub". Sucked down into some dank pit where no civilizing influence prevails. A place without reason, logic, order. A place where moans and groans replace language. *(a shy, deeply embarrassed transition)* There was, nearly always, ecstasy at the moment of entry. Jesus. What a cheap, bodice-ripping insult of a word. But that's what it was. And then I'd wait for a further heightening. *(small smile)* It was promised, after all, by Molly Bloom. Wait and wait — out on the periphery somewhere, looking on. Spectating. And when it was over there was more relief than satisfaction. *(in a sing-song)* Goodnight. Sleep well. Busy day tomorrow.

RUTH

(to the audience, as the stage darkens, highlighting her) I had the longest, thickest hair. It drove Cam MacMillan crazy. All the hockey players were after me, and not just bush league. A goalie pal of mine went direct from Saskatoon to the Toronto Maple Leafs. But then Cam came to see how little I knew and it spoiled our loving. *(on the verge of tears)* I never learned the whole alphabet. Still can't get past "K" without a headache comin' on.

RACHEL   *(to the audience, as the stage darkens, highlighting her)* I tried to write a poem about it once, years ago. I was thinking about my Master's. And about my grandmother, from Minsk, coming over in steerage, arriving at Ellis Island with my mother in her arms and lice in her hair. I was thinking about my degree, and what a great advance it was. But this was after sex, and I wrote:

> *JESSICA returns from the path. She pauses to listen, but does not "enter".*

The woman of 1960
Is the same as in 1860
And in two-thousand-sixty
It will be the same again.
She'll rise at dawn
And it will fall to her
To wash the semen from the sheets
And bear the child.

I never liked the mess and muck of it. I never liked my own primordial smells.

The lighting returns to normal.

JESSICA   I'm going to write about that, sometime.

RACHEL   *(astonished)* Really? Dear God, why?

JESSICA   It's evidence of evolution. Here's what I'd have said if I could have been at the Scopes trial. *(as if to a jury)* Gentlemen, in the beginning there was the sea. Certain creatures slithered out of it, onto the land, and as time went by flippers turned to paws and paws to hands. Dodos, dinosaurs, mastedons came and went. We lost our tails, our fangs, our horns, our fur. We got fire, the wheel, steel. But the human female never lost her deep sea smell. Chemists have tried, for centuries, to conceal it. They've given us potions to sanitize, deodorize, anesthetize. But it's too ancient for

JESSICA	(*continued*) camouflage. It is, gentlemen, your indisputable link to your slithering origins.
RACHEL	(*the disapproving "schoolmarm"*) Jessica, eventually, when you commit that to paper, it will want a little edit.
JESSICA	I don't think so. I think I'd let it fly, as is. (*brief pause*) She was right. I need to talk privately. (*to herself, amazed at the depth of her present feelings*) God, how I love that child.

JESSICA exits through the kitchen.

RUTH	I'll get on my knees tonight and pray that wee lass isn't pregnant.
RACHEL	Do you really believe someone listens?
RUTH	I do. I don't know why, because mostly He's tired and He's shut off his monitor. What about you?
RACHEL	I don't practice Judaism. I'm an agnostic.
RUTH	Agnostic. (*thinking*) Did Martin Luther start that one, too?
RACHEL	The word was introduced by a man called Thomas Huxley, in 1869. It means a...a...suspension of judgment in matters that can't be proved.
RUTH	I see. On the fence, then, about God.
RACHEL	Yes.
RUTH	What brought you to that conclusion?
RACHEL	When I was sixteen some cousins came over from Europe with terrible tales. Property being confiscated, Jews being rounded up and sent to work camps. I prayed mightily every day for a couple of years. Then I saw pictures of the death camps. Heaps of skeletons, gold from their teeth, their shoes, their spectacles. And just at that time I read one of Shakespeare's sonnets. He referred to

RACHEL   (*continued*) "deaf heaven". Deaf heaven not
hearing his cries. I thought, yes, indeed. Deaf,
blind, incapacitated heaven. I haven't prayed
since.

RUTH   Are you Jewish at all, then?

RACHEL   The traditions are ingrained, and the antennae are
always out. Sometimes I'll hear, from kids in an
alley somewhere, "kike", "yid", "hebe". You can
be an agnostic, but you can't be on the fence
when you hear those things.

RUTH   They hurt.

RACHEL   They are daggers to the heart.

*RACHEL allows exposure. RUTH,
very moved, tries to touch RACHEL.
RACHEL tightens up and recoils at the
prospect of being hugged.*

RACHEL   Excuse me. I'm sorry. That was a mawkish thing
to say.

*A light goes on in RACHEL. She
remembers something, allowing for a
quick change of subject.*

Estrous! That's it. Estrous. (*running to write it
down*)

RUTH   Pardon?

RACHEL   When you used the term, "barnyard years" — I
couldn't remember the word for it. The word that
describes sexual frenzy. The estrous cycle is
when the female mammal willingly accepts the
male.

RUTH   Uh huh. I see a lot of estrous cycle on T.V.

RACHEL   So do I.

RUTH

I thought you never watched.

RACHEL

From April 'till October, I live in my garden. I think that if God is evident anywhere, it's in gardens. I watch T.V. occasionally in the winter, but I'm appalled at the sex and violence.

RUTH

All the real sex and violence is on the National Geographic animal shows.

RACHEL

Do you think so?

RUTH

I know so. There's a wild boar in Africa, a wild male boar whose penis is shaped like a corkscrew.

RACHEL

I saw that show! The penis was about six inches long, and it — (*making a circling motion with her finger*) — spiralled. I was amazed!

RUTH

I couldn't take my eyes off it.

RACHEL

(*laughing*) To be perfectly candid, neither could I.

JESSICA marches in, angrily.

JESSICA

What a bloody farce it is!

RACHEL

What?

JESSICA

Motherhood. On Mother's day they give us lace hankies. I tell you, there aren't enough lace hankies in all of County Cork to wipe the tears of motherhood. (*brief pause*) I have two pieces of news. Bad and disastrous. The bad is that we're to be honoured this evening with a visit from Charles Whitman.

RACHEL

On his motorcycle?

JESSICA

No. His father's Mercedes. He's driving up from Greenwich.

RUTH

Is he comin' for dinner?

JESSICA	Yes. I can not, today, prepare a dinner for this twerp!
RUTH	If she's invited him, we'll have to.
RACHEL	Why was he expelled from Choate?
JESSICA	Marijuana.
RACHEL	He was caught, smoking it?
JESSICA	Selling it.
RACHEL	Oi. What's the disastrous?
JESSICA	(*slumping into a chair, afraid of both women's reactions*) She's refusing to go to Yale in September.
RACHEL	What? (*brief pause*) This can not be.
JESSICA	Charlie's father owns a farm in Colorado. He's sending the boy there, July first. Polly's going *with* him!
RUTH	(*incredulously*) "Polly's — going — with him"?
JESSICA	The dad wanted the boy to go to college, and then down to Wall Street. The boy's refusing both.
RACHEL	And you come out here like a dish rag, and lie down like a doormat, and say to me, Polly's going with him!
RUTH	To us, Rachel. She's saying it to us. (*almost attacking JESSICA*) What is the matter with you? Are you just caving in?
JESSICA	She looked so...formidable, when she told me. Perhaps, if Martin were here I'd be more —
RACHEL	Martin was no damned good! Martin bent over backward not to make waves.

JESSICA

Martin was a saint!

RACHEL

(*furiously*) Martin was shtupping some little bimbo on some enchanted evening while you were lecturing at Notre Dame!

> *JESSICA is astounded at this comment.*

JESSICA

Rachel!

RACHEL

I'm sorry! Oh, God, I'm sorry!

> *JESSICA, wounded, begins to exit.*

RACHEL

Please, forgive me —

JESSICA

(*whirling on RACHEL*) Rachel, I need to point out that *you* didn't listen to your mother — (*to RUTH*) And neither did you — and neither did I. Polly seems to be carrying on the tradition.

> *JESSICA exits, through the kitchen.*

RACHEL

She is utterly inept!

RUTH

Useless as tits on a bull.

RACHEL

(*pacing*) The girl is eighteen years old and about to wear, if not the royal purple, the bulldog blue, and she wants to go to Colorado, for Christ's sake! I can not tell you the folly I've witnessed in this house! All due to her lenience. They'd wheedle and whine. They'd plead and cajole. Latin was making life miserable. Calculus gave everybody migraine. Andy wanted out of basketball — he played like a klutz. Polly skipped piano — she had the cramps. Jess gets on the phone, prevaricates, goes to the principal, gets them off the hook. No Latin, no calculus, no basketball, no Mozart. But this. This I will not tolerate! (*moving to a position where she can holler up to POLLY's bedroom*) Polly Cohen, get your tushie down here on this deck this minute!

POLLY   (*offstage*) I can't!

RACHEL   (*to RUTH*) She can't.

RUTH   Oh, yes, she can! (*going to centerstage, hollering up to POLLY's bedroom*) Listen to me, you stupid little bitch! You can stay out all night long while we're convinced you've been axed into chunks and left piecemeal in the marsh! You can stand there like a brick shithouse and tell your mother you're throwing your life away on a dope peddlar with a foot-long dong! If you can't come down here in the next thirty seconds, I'm comin' up there and breaking your bloody neck.

POLLY   (*offstage*) I'll be down as soon as I shower.

                    Curtain.

Act Two, Scene One

*RACHEL paces on the deck,
"hyperventilating" slightly, waiting for
POLLY. RUTH and JESSICA are seen
moving about at the kitchen counter,
wearing aprons. JESSICA is making
stuffing, for chicken. An eight-pound
roaster sits nearby, in a roasting pan.
(Note: The roaster might possibly be
latex, and JESSICA might use a
prepared stuffing, such as "Pepperidge
Farm", adding chopped onions, parsley,
etc.) RUTH is peeling potatoes for
potato salad.*

*During the scene, the women fetch
items from the refrigerator, stop, and
listen. They go to drawers for knives,
peelers, etc., stop, listen, interject. The
work they perform is done with
intensity, but unthinkingly, by rote.
(The physical imperative of the opening
is that someone is coming to dinner and
a meal must be made) POLLY, freshly
showered, wearing a light summer robe,
enters the kitchen and sees that
RACHEL is waiting for her on the
deck. RACHEL makes half a gesture,
wanting to summon POLLY to the
deck. POLLY purposely avoids this
confrontation for a moment, addressing
JESSICA.*

POLLY	What are you fixing?
JESSICA	Stuffing. I had a roaster in the fridge for tomorrow. Gramma Cohen'll do a cheesecake and Gramma Mac's making potato salad.
POLLY	Thank you. I really appreciate this. I know it's last minute —
JESSICA	Missy, you know nothing.

> *POLLY now locks eyes with the waiting RACHEL. RACHEL crooks her finger, summons POLLY, and points at the floor in front of her. POLLY steels her courage and moves out to the deck.*

POLLY	Gramma Cohen, I'll try to be reasonable, but I won't undergo a Spanish Inquisition. I'm exhausted. I haven't slept.
RACHEL	Poor little pisher hasn't slept.
POLLY	(*eyeing the sandwiches*) And I'm hungry. I haven't eaten.
RACHEL	So eat.

> *POLLY gets a sandwich from the table. She addresses JESSICA, in the kitchen.*

POLLY	Are we doing hors d'oeuvres?
RUTH	Are we doing what?
JESSICA	Appetizers. Missy, you want appetizers, you come and make appetizers!
RACHEL	(*impatiently*) Please let's not have a megillah over appetizers! I'll do it. A little onion, a couple of chicken livers, no big deal. Bubelah, you had the highest —

RUTH	(*from the counter*) I want to know, lassie. Did you use a safe?
POLLY	A what?
JESSICA	A rubber!
POLLY	(*embarrassed and blushing*) Yes, he did.
RUTH	Hallelujah.
JESSICA	That's a relief!
RACHEL	If I prayed, I'd thank God.
RUTH	Where did you spend the night?
RACHEL	You know where. In a sleazy motel with paper bathmats.
POLLY	(*controlling herself*) Actually, we went out to North Guilford, to Meeting House Hill. We spent the night in the Congregational church.
RACHEL	It happened there, in the Congregational church?
POLLY	Yes.
RACHEL	Oi, on a pew made by Puritans.
POLLY	(*reasonably*) Afterwards, we talked and opened our hearts to each other. Then, at dawn, we sat on the hill by all those crooked gravestones, and planned a future.
RACHEL	In Colorado.
POLLY	Yes, on a farm.
RUTH	(*erupting*) A farm! That's what I can't swallow. You know what you are? You're a log jam in my river. (*moving out to the deck*) Rachel, I'm sorry — I'm interrupting — but a farm is what you get away from. (*to POLLY*) My mum wanted one

RUTH

(*continued*) thing — a brick house, because the Indians come and burned down wooden ones. She didn't get it. All I wanted was a Grade Eight diploma. I didn't get it. Your mum wanted a college degree. She didn't get it. But I did get off the farm, and your mum got off the prairie, and now you come along, slated for college with money in the bank, and you're a big log jam in my river — (*heading back to the counter*) — because you want to go back to a bloody, effing farm!

RACHEL

(*to RUTH*) Are you finished?

RUTH

For the moment. You know why I didn't get my Grade Eight diploma?

POLLY

Why?

RUTH

Because the horse froze.

JESSICA

Oh, Jesus.

RACHEL

I beg your pardon?

POLLY

What?

RUTH

I was in Grade Two. We went to school in a sleigh, me and three neighbour kids. One day it was forty below and the snow was ten feet deep and the horse got stuck. So we left that animal there, stiff as a poker and dead as a doornail, and he didn't thaw out until May. And, Polly, I was the oldest. Mum had four younger and she needed me at home. So she just said to hell with it, and kept me home. And you know what I become? A scullery maid for the whole damn family.

> *POLLY, exasperated, gazes out to the water.*

Don't drift on me, girl! You may think this is neither here nor there but, believe me, it's here, in me, it never leaves me.

POLLY	Gramma, I'm not a log jam. Mom didn't go to college and she's done very well. She owns this house, her name's on the deed, her book's in the window at the book store.
RUTH	Your mum was a prairie girl. She had gumption. You're a spoiled Yankee kid who wore braces on your teeth for two years. Your mum learned early on how to get up in the morning and do battle with the day.
RACHEL	And your dad was your mother's college education.
JESSICA	I beg your pardon? (*coming out of the kitchen*) Heavens, is that what you think?
RACHEL	You were right off the prairie. You'd had little exposure to anything. (*to POLLY*) Your dad plunked her down in Cambridge. Boston was at her doorstep, all their friends were intellectuals. Gerald harnassed whatever it was that forced the bud to bloom.
RUTH	(*defiantly*) Gerald might have harnassed it, but Cam MacMillan caused it. I seen four writers once, being interviewed on TV. They all said they got to be writers because of unhappy childhoods.

> *JESSICA, RUTH, RACHEL erupt and overlap each other, ad-libbing.*

JESSICA	Oh, for God's sake, Mum —
RUTH	That's what they said!
RACHEL	That is so simplistic —
JESSICA	Surely you don't —
POLLY	(*with slight irritation*) Ladies? Ladies, do I need to be here for this?

RACHEL   You do. I have plenty to say.

POLLY   (*to RACHEL*) I can see you've got yourself
              primed. You've obviously, all of you, made snap
              judgments about Charles without having one iota
              of real information. You're behaving as if he's
              some generic male. He isn't. If you knew the
              specifics you'd have great compassion.

RACHEL   Try me.

POLLY   Well, his name is Charles Allerton Whitman. He
              was born on Fifth Avenue, near 79th. His
              parents divorced when he was ten, and they
              dumped him into boarding school.

RACHEL   Where?

POLLY   (*getting a glass of lemonade*) Milford Academy.
              He's only seen his mother twice in the last ten
              years, and his dad plays polo in Brazil all winter.

RACHEL   Polly, these are the people I see in *Town and
              Country* Magazine! They look embalmed.

POLLY   Gramma —

RACHEL   I had an uncle who organized for the Garment
              Worker's Union. I had an aunt who was friendly
              with Red Emma Goldman. I had yet another
              uncle who couldn't work on Wall Street because
              the Whitmans of the world kept the Jews out.

POLLY   Gramma, I'm gonna keep my cool on this, but
              you're wrong to just dismiss rich people. It's just
              as wrong as, like, when somebody hears my
              name and they just dismiss me as Jewish.

JESSICA   Rachel, that is true.

POLLY	Charlie Whitman's really had tough sledding. He can't remember either parent ever being affectionate with him. There was never, ever, a Sunday breakfast when they all sat down to bacon and eggs. And, I mean, this is really wild. No one ever came to pick him up on holidays. He watched all the other boys drive off to decorate their Christmas trees, and he was the only kid left in the dorms. One Christmas Eve he, like, really steeled his courage and sent a telegram to his mother. He said, "Mom, it is very lonely here." You know what she replied? "Charles, it is lonely everywhere."
RUTH	Poor wee lad.
POLLY	(*to RUTH*) Gramma, the only place he's ever been happy is the farm. He's spent summers there all through his teens. He never gets into trouble out there because the work gives him a real sense of purpose. He's learned how to tan leather — (*to RACHEL*) and, I mean, I could just see the pride in his eyes when he talked about this vast, organic garden he's planted. I mean, this is no itty-bitty backyard plot, it's two whole acres that he tends himself. And he's, like, an apprentice to two men out there. One makes saddles and the other works with wood.
RUTH	Making furniture?
POLLY	Paddles.
RACHEL	Paddles?
POLLY	Hand-made paddles for rowing.
RUTH	For what?
POLLY	For sculls.
RUTH	For what?
JESSICA	Canoes, Mum, canoes!

RACHEL	Oi, gevalt. Saddles and paddles.
JESSICA	Polly, you have nothing in common with this boy! This is so whimsical, sweetie, so impulsive. Why can't the two of you go away somewhere, try being alone together for at least a couple of weeks?
POLLY	You mean, like, a test drive?
JESSICA	That's exactly what I mean. See what emerges. Find out what really makes him tick.
POLLY	I know that already.
RUTH & RACHEL	(*simultaneously*) Oh, yeah — Sure you do.
POLLY	Mama, it wouldn't help. It'd be, like, comparison shopping when I have no other model to compare. It'd be tense and awful, like, an exam. And wherever we went we'd be in artificial circumstances. I mean, where would we go? A sleazy motel with paper bath mats? What I have to do is convince all of you that I know, in my bones, that this is right. (*mood transition, about to broach the most painful thing in her young life*) We have everything in common, Mama. We couldn't be more in sync. We're both victims of divorce.
JESSICA	I beg your pardon? Victims? Did I ever abdicate responsibility? Did I ever deny you hugs and cuddles? Can you recall a single Sunday morning without bacon and eggs?
POLLY	I recall you and Dad asking Andy and me to go into the living room. And Charles recalls his mother and dad doing the same. And both you and Charlie's mother said, "We have something to tell you." (*beginning to cry*) It was, like, you dropped a guillotine on our lives. We thought you loved each other. We thought we were secure.

JESSICA	(*defensively*) Compared to this family you're describing, you have lived in a veritable Eden.
POLLY	I've lived, as has Charles, in a state of schism.
JESSICA	Schism?
POLLY	Yes! Shuttling back and forth to Berkeley —
JESSICA	Eden, Missy! Eden, compared with the way I was raised!

> *RACHEL, RUTH, and POLLY react
> simultaneously, more with groans than
> audible words.*

RUTH	Oh, boy.
RACHEL	Oi.
POLLY	Oh, God.
JESSICA	I peed my pants everytime my dad hit me! I was out working at eleven. And when I got home his golf clubs were gone to the bootlegger. Then the good china was gone, then, one day, the kitchen stove was gone! Because he had to have forty goddamned ounces of rye whisky every day!
POLLY	You forgot the door.
JESSICA	What?
POLLY	The night he removed the door from your closet, while the bootlegger waited down below.
JESSICA	You're a brazen little brat! When I told my dad that I wanted to go to college he said, "If you learn to type you don't even need Grade Twelve — you can go to work at sixteen." Jesus! If I'd gone to college my whole life would have been different. I spent my entire childhood asking my mother why the hell we stayed in that desperate situation.

RUTH   We stayed so's I could see that you got a high
            school diploma! (*to POLLY*) I dug in there and
            put up with crap you wouldn't believe so your
            mother could live in a decent house in a very
            good neighbourhood.

JESSICA   Oh, my God, "a very good neighbourhood"?

RUTH   Our neighbourhood, Mayfair, was very good!
            Ferguson, the lawyer, lived next door. The
            manager of the Bank of Montreal lived up the
            street. I wanted that for you.

JESSICA   (*furiously*) What did you want? What kind of
            drivel are you talking about? Are you saying you
            wanted me to have some kind of ludicrous...
            social symmetry...no matter how fearful the
            tempest behind the front door?

RUTH   Jessie, where could I go? What could I do?

RACHEL   Oi, yoi, yoi, yoi, yoi.

JESSICA   Surely more than what you did! Do you know
            what she did? She said, "When he hits you, head
            for your bedroom and fall on the bed." She said,
            "I'll whip in under him and pull up the
            eiderdown, and you won't feel the blow." (*to
            RUTH*) I can never forgive you for that!

RUTH   What I can't forgive you for would fill more
            books than they've got in that Silver Library you
            showed me at Yale!

JESSICA   Mother, it is called the Sterling Library!

RUTH   Well, maybe around here that's what it's called.

RACHEL   Are you finished?

RUTH   For the moment.

RACHEL   (*urgently*) Bubelah, you had the highest I.Q. in
          your class. You're on the National Honour Roll.
          You've aced the SAT's. And lest we forget, this
          isn't just college, it's Yale. We're not talking
          about Podunk U., y'know. Yale graduates stick
          together in a network that runs the country.
          Doors would open for you all your life. You
          know the Yale lock you buy at the hardware? I
          always thought it was an Ivy League lock — it's
          used to keep people out. That key is given to a
          privileged few. You can not summarily throw
          this away!

POLLY   Gramma, I'm eighteen. I can.

RACHEL   (*passionately*) Please, bubie, listen. I graduated
          from Podunk U., in Malvern. I wanted to work
          with books, to get into editing, but the New
          York publishers hired only Smithies and Cliffies.
          I called them tweed girls with paisley belly
          buttons. They knew about Bendel and Bonwit's.
          They knew about Mark Cross. The mothers
          belonged to the Colony Club and the fathers sat
          on the Stock Exchange. I had four sixteen-dollar
          outfits from Sears' catalogue. My father sat on a
          bench at the only kosher butcher shop in
          Malvern, Pennsylvania. If I had gone to an Ivy
          school my whole life would have been different!

RUTH   (*from the kitchen*) For God's sake, Rachel, you
          got two degrees — what're you griping about?

RACHEL   Ruth, it's my turn! My credentials didn't stand
          up. I got married and taught fifth grade and had
          three children. I was bored to tears, so I got a
          Master's and taught tenth grade. I lobbied for
          twelfth, but twelfth grade teachers, in those days,
          had another lock. A men's lock. Because twelfth
          grade teachers could become principals.

POLLY   Gramma, forgive me, but I have to say that you
          and Dad are really hung up on credentials.
          Diplomas, in Latin, that you can frame and hang

POLLY	(*continued*) on your walls. What is this obsession? Is it something Jewish?
JESSICA	I used to ask your dad that. He said that knowledge was the one thing the Jews could take with them, everytime they were banished.
RACHEL	Knowledge is simply a Jewish standard. It happens to be a more transportable commodity than land or money. It stands you in good stead whether you're banished, evicted, orphaned or widowed. You're avoiding the issue here —
POLLY	I'm not! I'm trying to find out why you and Dad are so —
RACHEL	O.K., O.K., let's pursue it. This Jewish standard is a lesson that would have served the Irish well — and the Italians and the Poles and the Slavs — my God, between 1880 and 1920, twenty-five million came to Ellis — not to mention four and a half million blacks brought in bondage before 1860 — not to mention the Mohawk and Huron and Blackfoot who were here in the first place. Did you find Jews on welfare, on assembly lines, in coal mines? If so, only momentarily. Why? Because —
JESSICA	Please, Rachel, spare us your list!
RUTH	What list?
JESSICA	Moses and Jesus— Einstein— Freud —
POLLY	Spinoza and Disraeli —
JESSICA	Einstein and Freud —
POLLY	Baruch and Bernstein —
JESSICA	Horowitz and Heifetz, Salinger and Singer, etc., etc., etc., — including Theda Bara on the silver screen.

RACHEL I am sometimes, on this subject, a little
predictable.

> *RACHEL sits down with POLLY and
> continues, sotto voce.*

Polly, I have a confession to make to you. And
you know, for me, such things don't come
easily. All through my marriage I fantasized. I
hated the routine, the muling, puking kids, the
tantrums, the endless preparation of meals — the
whole domestic travesty. Somewhere in your
brain you're thinking about babies, aren't you?
Little Whitman progeny. You know what
motherhood is? Motherhood is marathon feeding.
When I discovered that, I went to the library. I
went every Saturday and got seven books. One a
day, like vitamins, and I used those books as a
shield. And when my eyes gave out I fantasized.
Not the way my friends did, not for Gary Cooper.
My fantasies took me — you know where? (*a
brief, vulnerable pause, and change of tone*) To
Oxford. I wore flowing black robes. I walked
with dons. I made friends with beadles. I spent
balmy afternoons in the Bodleian. (*gazing out
dreamily*) I even had engraved stationery in this
fantasy. "Rachel Kaufman Cohen, Merton
College, founded 1264." (*pausing, deeply
embarrassed, then to RUTH*) Are you finished
there, Ruth?

RUTH I am.

RACHEL I'd better start my cheesecake.

RUTH (*moving out to POLLY, quickly*) Lassie, listen.
I do remember my barnyard years, and my long,
thick hair, and my heat. I see that heat all over
you today. But Polly, this heat lasts about as
long as hiccups. And then, when things turn bad,
you can't get out. You have to be able to get out!
If you've put all your eggs in one basket you've
got no choices, no skills, no money —

> *RACHEL erupts in anger. During RACHEL's following speech, JESSICA becomes increasingly impatient.*

RACHEL   What you don't have, in summation, is any damned clout in the world! Jesus! Every Thursday night I go to my book club. Ten of us have been trying to decipher *Finnegan's Wake* for as long as I can remember. Afterward, in what is ostensibly the discussion period, all we do is talk about ourselves. Ten old liver-spotted, stretch-marked, tit-sagging ladies nattering about what we did in the past, what we didn't do, what we should have done. How differently it would have turned out *if only*. When I get home, I swear, I'm ready to take a razor to my wrists. What we want you to do, Polly, is learn from us! Gird yourself now, against a life of what-ifs and should-haves and all-consuming regret.

POLLY   Gramma, that's impossible! (*erupting, moving away swiftly*) God, how can someone so logical even ask that?

JESSICA   (*grabbing POLLY*) Sweetie, *all that matters*, and I've said it for twenty years, is meaningful work.

POLLY   That's not what you've said for twenty years. You've always said that two things matter. The first is loving someone deeply and the second is meaningful work. You've forgotten the first because Charles happens not to be Ethan Kendall.

JESSICA   I've forgotten the first because I...Oh, Polly. I was packing Martin's things this morning and I discovered, well....evidence that he betrayed me.

POLLY   (*very concerned*) Oh, Mom, no. (*embracing JESSICA*)

JESSICA   Yes.

POLLY   (*in disbelief*) Not Martin.

JESSICA   I believe he found someone, albeit briefly, and
                told her all my secrets. I'm sure of it. (*brief
                pause*) Polly, today, for the first time really, I
                understand "Nina" in Chekhov's *Seagull*. Do you
                remember the play?

POLLY   Yes.

RACHEL   Have you read it?

POLLY   Uh huh.

RACHEL   What did you think of it?

POLLY   Well, you know Chekhov. Talk, talk, talk.

RACHEL   Kvetch, kvetch, kvetch.

JESSICA   Darling, at the end, Nina comes home. She left
                very young, very naive, and she's had an
                illegitimate child. She comes home worn-out and
                heartbroken. And she says to Kostia, "I think
                now I know that what matters is work. Not fame
                or glamour, but knowing how to endure."

                Darling, you must, somehow, find work that
                sustains you. Because life is so difficult, sweetie.
                People are frail and petty and disappointing.
                Loved ones die — we're afflicted unexpectedly
                with what George Eliot called "the shaft of
                disease". Households break up, kids end up in
                comas, and since the beginning of time there's
                either been war, or it's in the planning stage. All
                that's changed is the weaponry. (*passionately*)
                Darling babe, it doesn't have to be highbrow, or
                longhair, or creative. Remember how you used to
                go down to Fair Street and watch that man repair
                antique clocks? He loved the little gear trains and
                balance wheels, he loved the burl of the wood.
                He was oblivious to the world — he didn't even
                know you were there. I thank —

RACHEL   Chisel the point, Jessica, chisel the point!

JESSICA   I thank God that He's given me access to that kind of oblivion! Two weeks ago I lived here with Martin in what I thought was a holy alliance. A week from now both of your Grammas will be gone — you, too, may be gone. I'll go back to the only refuge I have. Back into my head, into my work.

>   *POLLY's head falls and she begins to cry.*

Sweetiekins, what's the matter?

POLLY   I don't want to be oblivious to the world. I have no reason to be.

RACHEL   As yet, Polly. As yet.

POLLY   (*crying openly for a moment*) Jesus! This is like visiting a musty old room full of damp and decay. An airless, mildewed room. (*pause, controlling herself*) I think I've behaved well. I vowed that I would, and I have. I've sat here and listened. But everything I've heard is about breakdown and failure.

RACHEL   (*sadly*) That is, unfortunately, our frame of reference.

POLLY   But you think you're wise and experienced and you're really just old and cynical. And you've all fiddled with the truth in order to make your decisions acceptable. I mean, like, your visions of yourselves are really warped. Gramma Mac, you love to talk about gumption. Pioneer stock and prairie persistence. All I've heard, since I came out of the womb, is that you can't read. Where was your gumption when you left the farm? Why didn't you get yourself into a class?

RUTH   I did! An English class.

POLLY   Did you? When?

RUTH	When I met your grandpa. I put on my best dress, and I wore my Egyptian cotton gloves that cost a fortune. And when I got in there I was the only woman, and the room was full of foreigners.
POLLY	So?
RUTH	They were immigrants! They had to learn to say, "Good morning".
POLLY	So?
RACHEL & JESSICA	(*simultaneous reprimands*) Polly! Missy!
RUTH	I could talk a blue streak, I just couldn't read. It was insulting to be there, so I quit.
POLLY	Well, O.K., you quit. But, Gramma — this just makes me nuts. You're almost proud when you say that Grandpa MacMillan's cruelty caused Mom to write.
RUTH	Well, it did. I see the proof in *The Saskatoon Star Pheonix.*
POLLY	The what?
RUTH	The newspaper. Everytime she writes a book they put her picture in the paper. The girls who grew up normal — the girls who went to proms and got corsages and married Anglican — they don't ever get their pictures in the paper.
POLLY	I can't believe this. God, what a cop out! Grandpa never hit you, did he? He saved all his rage for Mom, who was really helpless.
RUTH	She wasn't helpless! She learned long words real quick. She give him as good as she got.

POLLY
If Charles Whitman ever treats a child of ours like that, I'll run a fuckin' knife through him.

RUTH
How can you say she was helpless? If you'd heard 'em, goin' at it tooth and nail, you'd know that she held her own.

POLLY
Gramma, you've told me that, and Mom's told me that, but Mama had words and Grandpa had fists.

RUTH is visibly stung. A pause.

RUTH
I want to go home.

POLLY
Gramma Cohen, you've spent your whole life wanting to be someone else, somewhere else, wearing some other clothes.

RACHEL
(*angrily*) Because I had aspirations! Lofty aspirations. Not to be a Jewish princess. Not to spend my life adorning myself and then going to spas and eating Bibb lettuce to make the adornments fit. Head aspirations! (*tapping her forehead*) Grey matter!

POLLY
But you've succeeded! Why do you have to master everything so ferociously? Why do you behave as if you'll be spanked if you don't measure up? Gramma, I've seen you, like, really lose it when you leave a blank in a crossword puzzle.

RACHEL
I never leave a blank.

POLLY
You did on Wednesday. When I went to bed Wednesday night there were blanks in the puzzle.

RACHEL
Because I couldn't remember "ret". (*spelling it*) Are-Eee-Tee. It means to soak flax. I remembered it at midnight and got up and finished the puzzle. You should have checked on Thursday.

POLLY   Oi, gevalt! Will you admit that you've lived your whole life vicariously?

RACHEL   For Chrissake, what is this? Why are you putting *us* through a Spanish Inquisition?

POLLY   Why have you had to hide in other people's experiences, in books?

RACHEL   Because I'm afraid. Is that so complicated? Books give me safety in distance. Books give me information without the suffering.

POLLY   God, you're just like Dad.

RACHEL   Because we know that when you're all passion, and pathos—and you happen not to be a writer who spews it out on paper—the world uses you up and dumps you at the curb.

RACHEL is visibly stung.

JESSICA   Polly, please, enough! You really are overstepping the —

POLLY   Mama, you and Gramma Cohen wonder why you're still so connected after the divorce. You're the other side of Gramma's coin. She hides in reading, you hide in writing.

JESSICA   I do not hide!

POLLY   You do. It's your way of holding the world at bay.

JESSICA   It is not! I create. I express myself!

POLLY   After the divorce you went into your study and closed the door. That is *my* frame of reference.

JESSICA   For God's sake, I wasn't evading anything! I was grappling with the goddamn economics of single-parenthood. I had, suddenly, to earn a living with my pen!

POLLY   But that was your choice. You're the one who wanted the divorce.

JESSICA   You've never forgiven me for that, have you? You've always implied that, because I refused to live a life of emotional paralysis, I was the spoiler. That it was, somehow, my hubris that caused the break-up. Missy, let me tell you what really galls me! You grew up with lots of kids who were "victims of divorce". But in every case the mother had been abandoned by a father who'd run off with a younger woman. You found that excusable. You bought into that old chestnut that men are tomcats and women are long-suffering. Let me tell you, Missy, you bought into a load of chauvinistic bullshit!

POLLY   But you were long-suffering.

JESSICA   I have never had one moment of regret about the divorce!

POLLY   But you've had an abundance of guilt. Because, hard as you tried, you couldn't compensate for the loss of Dad. Hard as you tried you couldn't really cope with single-parenthood. And God, you did try hard! You were like a whirling-dervish with your devotion.

JESSICA   This is outrageous!

POLLY   Bacon and eggs, hugs and cuddles — it was suffocating. You know what we called it, Andy and I? "Smothering mothering."

JESSICA   (*stunned*) We are not going to stand here and take this any longer! We, all of us, have done the best we could, given the circumstances.

POLLY   All I want is to do the same! (*brief pause*) I refuse to believe that misery is inevitable. I'm not Nina. I don't have an illegitimate child, I'm not worn-out, I'm not heartbroken. I'm eighteen, and I'm filled with hope and anticipation. I've met a wonderful boy who just — invades my heart. I'm counting the minutes until I see him again. Between now and then I can't, do you hear me — I can not listen to one more moment of your carefully nurtured sorrows. (*beginning to exit, then pausing*) And when Charles gets here, will you please, all three of you, lighten up a little?

                POLLY exits through the kitchen. RUTH, RACHEL and JESSICA, all wounded, are in silent tableau for a moment. RACHEL and JESSICA move to gather the lunch plates and glasses. Then RACHEL turns to RUTH with a safe, cold, irrefutable fact.

RACHEL   Ruth, Meeting House Hill — where they went — is very historical. Late Seventeenth century. (*to JESSICA*) Isn't Harriet Beecher Stowe buried on Meeting House Hill?

                RACHEL and JESSICA have the following exchange, as if by rote. It is their habitual way of holding pain at bay.

JESSICA   No, her mother is.

RACHEL   I thought she lived in Guilford.

JESSICA   She was born here, but she wrote *Uncle Tom's Cabin* somewhere else.

RACHEL   Where?

JESSICA   I don't know.

RACHEL   We'll have to look it up.

JESSICA	Yes. Yes, we will.
RUTH	I want to go home.
JESSICA	You can't.
RUTH	No, not yet.

Curtain.

Act Two, Scene Two

It is seven o'clock the same night.
RUTH wears a pretty, slightly formal,
cotton dress under an apron. This, her
"airplane" dress, must have pockets. She
stands down front, looking quizzically
toward the neighbouring property.
RACHEL, wearing a hand-woven, hand-
dyed smock, under an apron, is in the
kitchen. She is spreading her chopped
chicken liver on large crackers.
RACHEL is barefoot: her shoes are
nearby, under a table. (NOTE: The
following are activities that JESSICA,
RACHEL and RUTH might utilize
during parts of the scene. They put
candles in candlesticks, fetch a large
platter to hold the chicken, a gravy boat
to hold gravy, a bowl to hold stuffing, a
carving knife. They put nuts in a bowl,
butter in a butter dish. They slice
French bread and put it in a basket.
They set out dessert plates and put sugar
in a bowl, cream in a creamer. Someone
might toss a green salad, someone
might arrange a small bowl of flowers,
a "centerpiece")

RUTH   That handsome Peter's out on the rocks again.
Wait a minute. There's a dark, hairy man joining
him.

RACHEL   That's his friend, Mark.

RUTH

Peter looks like a movie star. Is his wife beautiful, too?

RACHEL

There's no wife. Mark is...the wife.

RUTH

(*wide-eyed, after a moment*) Fruits?

RACHEL

Ruth, around here we say "gays."

RUTH

Rachel, let's get this straight. Around here isn't everywhere. (*brief pause*) The other one looks like something the cat drug in. And he's twenty years older.

RACHEL

And he's Jewish. (*a devilish smile*) I call them Sodom and Menorah. (*laughing heartily*)

RUTH

Is that funny?

RACHEL

I think so.

RUTH

Can you explain it?

RACHEL

(*coming down from the counter*) Well, uh, there were these two ancient cities, Sodom and Gomorah. (*looking at RUTH, no response*) Uh, let's see. In the Jewish religion there's this thing, like, a candelabrum. It's called a menorah. (*looking at RUTH, no response*) No, I can't explain it.

JESSICA, wearing a summer cotton dress, enters. She carries an old snapshot album. She puts it down and puts on an apron.

RUTH

Well, now, that's pretty.

JESSICA

Thank you.

RUTH

Am I too gussied up, do you think, in my airplane dress?

JESSICA

Not at all.

RACHEL	When's he due?
JESSICA	Seven-thirty.
RUTH	What time is it now?
JESSICA	Seven-fifteen. Polly's still getting ready.
RACHEL	Apparently it takes two hours.
RUTH	I saw her leaving the kitchen with a saucepan! What on earth is she doing?
JESSICA	Waxing her legs. (*pause, her voice falters*) I can't do this.
RUTH	What?
JESSICA	I can't, can not, sit at that table and make chat with a feckless youth.
RACHEL	You can and you will. (*urgently, almost pouncing on JESSICA*) Jess, I have a desperate feeling that I am Custer and this is the last stand. It's absolutely imperative that we have one last stab at the boy.
JESSICA	No, Rachel. No, no —
RACHEL	A delicate stab. After dinner. No emotion, no histrionics, a mere suggestion that he get a job in New Haven while Polly attends Yale for one year.
JESSICA	He can't get a job, he has no training!
RACHEL	He can do what all the other untrained masses do! He can sling hash at McDonald's, or Burger King, or Kentucky Fried.
JESSICA	It's a bad idea. I haven't the energy.
RACHEL	We have the energy. (*to RUTH*) Haven't we?

RUTH   We have. And it don't have to be delicate. He
                  should be sat down and talked turkey to. If, at the
                  end of a year, their heat lasted longer than
                  hiccups, they can go with our blessing. If not,
                  she'll stay in school and be grateful we didn't let
                  her flush her future down the crapper.

RACHEL   Exactly.

JESSICA   I forbid you to do this.

RACHEL   (*angrily*) Her father would do it, if he were here!
                  You, in fact, should do it, and you would, if the
                  strain of the last week hadn't left you a
                  gelatinous mess. So it's up to me. *In loco
                  parentis.*

JESSICA   You may find this presumptuous, but I do know
                  my daughter best. There are several good reasons
                  why you mustn't do this.

RACHEL   Try me.

JESSICA   (*struggling*) I just can't, at the moment, rally my
                  thoughts!

RACHEL   Rally, Jessica, rally! If you don't, I'm doing my
                  Custer number on that boy.

JESSICA   Ladies, I may be a gelatinous mess, but she is
                  intractable. (*to RACHEL*) If we have *at* the boy,
                  as you suggest, it'll look like an onslaught from
                  the Gang of Three — it'll send her directly
                  upstairs to pack. (*to RUTH*) If we talk the kind
                  of turkey you suggested, it'll be taken as an
                  ultimatum. She'll march to the phone, call the
                  travel agent, and book the trip.

RACHEL   Not if you explain that —

JESSICA	If she did go to school, leaving Charlie standing over boiling oil, frying fries, she would immediately enter into the state she is wont to call her "deep melancholia." She'd languish in a freshman dorm and her grades would hover around F. And Gerald and I would be coughing up three thousand dollars a month for room, board, tuition, tranquilizers and psychiatrists, for the privilege of having our daughter at Yale. (*brief pause*) No. Emphatically, no. It would be much better to take the opposite tack. Let her try the farm for a year. If it doesn't work she'll come home, hat in hand, not yet twenty, ready to hit the books. Yale's been there since 1716 — it isn't going to go away. I hate to pull rank but this is my daughter, my house, and it's my money, Mum, that she'd flush down the crapper. (*going back to the counter to perform a task*) So we will not have a last stab at the kid. Is that agreed?
RUTH	(*after a moment*) All right.
RACHEL	(*shrugging*) If you say so.
JESSICA	I said so.
RUTH	What time is it?
JESSICA	Seven-twenty-five. (*to RACHEL*) Did you put on the crystal goblets?
RACHEL	Nope, the ones from that "Pottery Barn" place.
JESSICA	(*beginning to exit*) Oh, for God's sake —
RACHEL	Why didn't you say you wanted crystal?
JESSICA	Did I have to? The kid's from Greenwich, for God's sake!

*JESSICA exits to the dining room.
RUTH returns to a task, RACHEL
removes her apron.*

RUTH   She's "Puttin' on the Ritz."

                  *RACHEL, fit to be tied, huffs, puffs
                  and paces.*

RACHEL   Oi, yoi, yoi, yoi, yoi.

RUTH   Rachel, that — what you're doing — is bad for
                  high blood pressure.

RACHEL   I know, I know.

RUTH   What do they call that, what you're doing?

RACHEL   Hyperventilating.

RUTH   Rachel, I have a thought I'd like to tell you, but
                  I'm scared.

RACHEL   Scared of me?

RUTH   A little. You have thoughts a mile a minute, and
                  you might think mine's stupid.

RACHEL   I think you have very keen insights. Please, tell
                  me.

RUTH   Well, the world irks you something awful, don't
                  it?

RACHEL   The people in the world.

RUTH   Because the people still do all the things the
                  Bible says "thou shalt not do".

RACHEL   Yes.

RUTH   Well, people haven't changed since they got up
                  off all fours.

RACHEL	Oh, I can't agree with that. It's anathema to — it's — it's against everything I stand for. God, look at our progress! We've had men on the moon, we've got men taking pictures of Mars, we've got men in laboratories cloning genes in test-tubes —
RUTH	That's science. There's no progress in humans.
RACHEL	But we've had great music, great literature —
RUTH	Why, Rachel, why were those commandments written in the first place?
RACHEL	Well, I guess — there was a need.
RUTH	Bingo. We were out of control then, and we still are. Everytime a kid is born we start from zero. That's my thought.

JESSICA enters, going to the counter to finish a task.

JESSICA	The table looks much better.
RACHEL	(*finding the crossword*) I hope Charles Allerton Whitman was advised that this is black-tie.
RUTH	Jess, take out that potato salad, will you? It's better at room temperature. What time is it now?
JESSICA	Seven-thirty.
RACHEL	I don't imagine punctuality is his strong suit. (*at the crossword*) Damn, I should know this. "To mimic", in three.
JESSICA	To mimic in three. Ape?
RUTH	An ape's a monkey.
RACHEL	(*writing it in*) Not in this case.

RUTH

Here's what I don't know about reading. There's a flower in a vase and there's flour in a bin. There's a kernel in the corn and a colonel in the army. There's a serial on the radio and there's cereal from Kellogg's. There's a carrot in the garden and a karat in a ring.

JESSICA

(*to RACHEL*) Those are homophones, aren't they?

RACHEL

Yes, indeedy.

JESSICA

(*to RUTH*) When they're spelled differently but pronounced identically, they're called homophones.

RUTH

How do you know that?

JESSICA

Gerald told me.

RACHEL

(*victoriously*) Ah ha! I rest my case.

JESSICA

I was going through the album this afternoon. Look at this. This is when she ran away from home.

RUTH

Ran away where?

JESSICA

She brought home a whole litter of kittens, and I refused to keep them, and she said in that case she'd go and live with Gramma Cohen.

RUTH

Why is she standing with two policemen?

JESSICA

They found her on I-95, on the other side of New Haven. She told them she was walking to Pennsylvania. I never remember the funny, tender little things until I look at the album.

RACHEL

This is why Kodak makes millions.

RUTH

What do you remember other times?

JESSICA	Smothering mothering. Running all day, frantically, like a gerbil on a wheel. Going to bed each night in defeat.
RACHEL	Why defeat?
JESSICA	Because during the day, while I was running, I'd glance to the right and the left and all I saw was unmet needs. Soul needs.
RACHEL	I hope you don't mean that in a religious context.
JESSICA	Of course not. I mean personalities. Burgeoning, baffling personalities. Moods, sulks, pouts — a maze of childhood frailties.
RUTH	What they want then, is tender, loving care.
RACHEL	(*bridling*) What they need then is discipline.
JESSICA	(*going back to a task*) Ah, Rachel. This is our old battle zone.
RACHEL	I found the pouts and sulks insufferable. I remember writing a letter to my sister. I said, "I am, unfortunately, finding these children quite infantile."
JESSICA	Rachel, what was the dominant feeling for you, in mothering?
RACHEL	Duty. One had to rise to the occasion.
JESSICA	I wanted to make the house a fortress and pen them in. Protect them from all exposure — oppressive heat, killing frosts, and most importantly, mirrors. Mirrors where they'd make that first, indelible judgment of themselves and wear it like a shackle, to their graves.
RACHEL	What time is it?

JESSICA   Seven-forty. Yipes. Let's see, we'll need dessert plates. (*as she gets them*) You know, I can only remember two or three occasions when there was pure, unqualified joy.

RUTH   There was joy for me when you were born, Jess. I thought you'd be my salvation. I thought you'd teach me to read. (*pause*) You hurt me terrible.

JESSICA   (*very surprised*) I did?

RUTH   Surely you remember.

JESSICA   No, I don't.

RUTH   I waited 'till third grade and then, one day, you come home and threw your books on the kitchen table. You were nine years old. I said, "Jessie, if you'd give me half an hour every day after school, maybe it's not too late for me to read." You were mean.

JESSICA   Mean? Was I?

RUTH   You said, "Mum, you're supposed to learn this when you're nine".

        JESSICA is stunned at this recollected cruelty.

JESSICA   I said that? Is that what you can't forgive me for?

RUTH   Yes.

JESSICA   (*going to RUTH, hugging her*) I'm sorry. I'm very, very sorry. I was insensitive.

RUTH   You were mean. And you don't even remember it.

JESSICA   Mum, I was nine.

RUTH	(*abruptly*) Oh, go away! (*brief pause*) Bloody scullery maid for the whole damn family when I was nine.
JESSICA	(*to RACHEL*) How can I take that back? How can I erase it from our slate?
RACHEL	If only we could.

JESSICA moves out of the scene. Lighting change to highlight RACHEL and RUTH together.

It's a painful business, thinking back through our mothers.

RUTH	It is. I wonder why?
RACHEL	Because they give us, quite literally, their blood. And in return we give them short shrift. It's a pattern as old as a subject and a predicate. (*brief pause*) My mother always carried a five dollar bill in her shoe. She said she wanted something in reserve for stormy weather. I hated watching her every morning — watching her bend and put the bill in her shoe. (*with difficulty*) One day I said, "It's your immigrant mentality that makes you do that." (*brief pause*) I said each word purposely, hurling my little javelins of perfect English into her Yiddish protests. When she died, I wanted more than anything to wipe that from our slate. I took her petticoat and dress to the undertaker, and with them five dollars that I put in her shoe. I thought I might achieve, in that action, atonement. But once the stinging sentence is uttered, one is sentenced to carry it all through one's life.
RUTH	(*to RACHEL*) I broke my mother's heart when I left the farm. It was October, threshing time. We had three hundred acres, and it was before combines, so seventeen men come with a steam outfit and stayed a whole week to take off the

RUTH   (*continued*) crop. An engineer, a fireman, a separator, a waterman, one man hauled the grain, eight men with teams of horses, four spike-pitching in the field. Mum and I butchered hogs and fried up thirty-four pork chops for their breakfast. We made ten loaves of bread every day for their sandwiches — in hundred degree heat in a woodstove. We went to bed at one a.m. and got up at four-thirty. We gave the men our beds, and one night I was beside my mum on the floor in the kitchen. I said, "Soon as threshing's over, I have to get out." "Why?", she asked. I said, "because I'm eighteen. And I've got callouses on my hands, corns on my toes, and I'm developin' housemaid's knee." I went into Saskatoon and got a job sewin' linings in fur coats. And I never went back. (*brief pause*) Our neighbourhood, Mayfair, was very good.

    POLLY comes in. She is nervous and anxious. She wears baggy cotton overalls over an attractive white shirt, and what appear to be men's boots.

POLLY   Hi.

RACHEL   For this you waxed your legs?

POLLY   Uh huh. (*checking her watch*) Seven-forty-five. Everything all set?

JESSICA   Almost.

POLLY   You look very nice.

RACHEL,
JESSICA,
& RUTH   Thank you.

POLLY   (*to RACHEL*) Gramma, you do intend to wear —

RACHEL   Shoes. I do. They're over there.

POLLY   Did you chill some wine?

JESSICA	Of course.
POLLY	I'd like to ask you, please, not to ask him what his father does, or how long he's lived in Greenwich.
RACHEL	(*facetiously*) I thought I'd ask him if he is now, or has ever been, a Communist.

RUTH and JESSICA laugh.

POLLY	Gramma, this is serious. He has a very, very slight limp from a bad skiing accident.
RACHEL	Too much schussing at Gstaad.
POLLY	Gramma, he had multiple fractures. Please, don't notice it.
JESSICA	We won't.
POLLY	And the future. If you must discuss the future, please, please, don't talk like guidance counsellors and suggest career opportunities. Please accept that the farm is final.
RUTH	What can we ask him?
POLLY	You could tell him about your prairie farm. He'd like that.
RUTH	You know I hated everything about the farm.
POLLY	What did you hate most?
RUTH	Makin' soap. Sifting the ashes from the wood, mixing 'em with lime, boiling 'em with grease and lye.
POLLY	That is so interesting! Please, tell him that when he comes. It's going to be so awkward at first, and that would, like, give us an opener. (*brief pause*) God, my palms are sweating.

RUTH

Imagine his. Imagine havin' to walk in here and meet all of us.

RACHEL

It shouldn't be too daunting. We're all eminently presentable.

RUTH

That's true. It's not like we're your Samuel Becket people, sitting around in ash cans.

POLLY

(*checking her watch*) Damn him! He's twenty minutes late.

JESSICA

He'll be fashionably late. Just after eight, I'd imagine.

POLLY

Of course, he won't be at his best tonight because there's tension. I mean, I know the dinner will be wonderful, and you'll all try and put him at ease, but still, there is stress. How could there not be? He'll probably make small, cautious utterances. I say this to forewarn Mom and Gramma Cohen, because you're both so judgmental about the use of the language.

RACHEL

I'm sure it'll be just fine.

POLLY

It won't, actually, because he's got a great gift of gab, and he uses lovely imagery — he even likes to use alliteration. (*pause*) I have a slight headache.

JESSICA

How did he use alliteration?

POLLY

He said, "pretty Polly's a paragon of perfection." (*looking to RACHEL, for approval*) Well?

RACHEL

Pretty Polly's a paragon of perfection is, perhaps, a little purple. (*a mood transition*) How did you meet him? Did someone introduce you?

POLLY   No, he was just there. You know what I mean?
Just fatefully there. As long as I live, I'll never
forget his overture. I wrote it down, verbatim, in
my diary this afternoon. I'd been aware of him
looking at me for a long, long time. Then he
came across the gym and he said, in a deep
baritone, (*in a baritone*) "You're the one." I said,
"You mean for the next dance?". (*in a baritone*)
"No", he said, "for life." God, it was dramatic!
And then he smiled and he had dimples. I've been
looking for dimples like that since I was twelve.

*During the following speech, POLLY
goes down front, to sit. JESSICA is
now placed apart from the other actors.
Lighting change to highlight JESSICA
as she gazes at her daughter.*

JESSICA   (*to herself*) Never again, for me. Fini. Oh,
somewhere down the line I may put on the peek-
a-boo. I'll open the menu and look across at him,
above a squat white candle and a tall pink
carnation, and I'll say, "Are the snails good
here?" But later, over brandy, when he reaches for
my hand, I'll be obliged to say, "I'm afraid there's
been a mistake. You have the false impression
that you're out to dinner with a woman. You
don't know that I've become neuter. You don't
know that you are, in fact, dining tonight with a
female impersonator."

Lighting change to highlight RACHEL.

RACHEL   (*to herself*) Aaron and I hardly had a perfect
marriage, but we found a lot of comfort in each
other. We drove to Philadelphia, to hear the
symphony. Saturday afternoons we listened to
the opera. We gardened together. In spring we'd
go out for walks, after dinner, and there'd be a
pervasive perfume from the blossoming trees,
and I'd take his arm.

JESSICA   (*still apart from the others*) Spring. Oh, God.

                         Lighting change to highlight RUTH.

RUTH   (*to herself*) I never dreamed I'd end up eating T.V. dinners in an aluminum tray. I still holler for him, when I'm moving something and I need a hand. I thought of him a week ago, at the airport. I walked out on that runway and I said to Heaven, "Cam? Can you see me? I'm gettin' on an air-O-plane. If it crashes and burns I'll be up there, on your doorstep, later in the day."

                         Lighting change to highlight POLLY.

POLLY   (*rising, addressing the audience*) Secretly, I'm prepared to admit that Charles Whitman is a rescue mission. Somebody has to kill that boy with kindness. I have absolute confidence that I can make him straighten up and fly right.

                         Lighting change to highlight RACHEL.

RACHEL   (*to herself*) On Aaron's sixtieth birthday we had a party. Afterward, we were alone, and the talk rolled around to death. I tried to avoid it — I despise sepulchral talk. I said, "What's to discuss? Our little lives are rounded with a sleep." I said I wanted to die in my garden with my shears in hand, and on my tombstone it should say, "Mostly, she'll miss delphiniums." Then Aaron said, "I know exactly when I want to die. The day after you."

                         Lighting change to highlight POLLY.

POLLY   (*to the audience*) Charlie Whitman's been pushed from pillar to post. He's had no ballast in his life. What he needs is a tranquil home where he can go to mend the day's damages. I won't do anything nouveau or trendy in furnishings. I'll do cheap and cheerful. (*continuing, dreamily*) I'm

POLLY

(*continued*) very partial to stripes. In wallpaper. But I think I'll have only floral upholstery. And potted plants. On carved, Chinese plant stands. And somewhere I'd like to have a window seat with a southern exposure. And a gazebo in the yard. (*frowning*) I wonder. Do farms have yards? Or is it all just....farm? And eventually I'll have stationery of my own. "Mrs. Charles Allerton Whitman, Rural Route number Four, Leslie, Colorado."

> *A pause. Lighting change back to normal. POLLY addresses all three.*

If I asked you to tell me, in one sentence, the secret of a lasting marriage, what would you say?

> *Brief pause.*

JESSICA

You should have souls that run parallel.

> *Brief pause.*

RACHEL

You should be well-matched at Scrabble.

> *Brief pause.*

RUTH

You should have your own, private money, in your own account.

> *RUTH sits down to her crocheting.*

JESSICA

Dear me. Eight-o-five.

POLLY

I'm feeling quite nauseous. Oh, God, what if he doesn't come?

RUTH

He probably got lost in one of the coves nearby.

POLLY

I gave him very good directions.

RACHEL

I think I'll baste the bird. (*going to the kitchen*) Where do you keep the ladle?

JESSICA	In the drawer left of the sink.
RACHEL	Such a Jewish word, ladłe. Ladle, dreydl, meydl, kneydl.
POLLY	Let's just admit it! He isn't coming.
RACHEL	Stop that! Of course he is!
POLLY	(*tensely, to JESSICA*) Why didn't you use the big, appliquéd tablecloth?
JESSICA	For God's sake, you've always said that tablecloth was positively Victorian! I used your favourite placemats.
POLLY	Placemats are just not appropriate! I'm going to put it on.
JESSICA	Go ahead. God forbid we should do anything inappropriate!

POLLY exits, in a huff.

RUTH	(*referring to her crocheting*) Jess, by next summer, if I live, you'll have this cloth for your table.
JESSICA	Yes. (*mournfully*) But who will be here to dine?
RACHEL	(*echoing JESSICA*) "But-who-will-be-here-to-dine?"
JESSICA	Do I detect a note of ridicule?
RACHEL	Not at all. But the question's a candidate, isn't it, for your future list of "carefully nurtured sorrows?"

> *RACHEL, finished basting, returns to the deck.*

JESSICA It probably is.

RACHEL I was wrong before. Shakespeare wouldn't have us dancing around a cauldron. He'd put us in a forest — those woods he longs for in — uh — mmm...Oh, God — *Two Gentlemen of Verona.* Ruth, in that play he wants to find a place where he can sit alone and — (*turning out, to the audience*) — "tune his distresses, and record his woes".

> *They change positions. Lighting changes may be made here, and music may be played under the following "litany of sorrows."*

RUTH If I'd have gotten Grade Eight my whole life would have been different.

JESSICA If I'd gone to college my whole life would have been different.

RACHEL If I'd gone to an Ivy school my whole life would have been different.

> *Brief pause, slight position change.*

RUTH I saw 'em out tilling, once. Mum and Dad with a hand-hewn plough and two big Percheron horses.

RACHEL When I was sixteen, some cousins came over from Europe.

RUTH I said, "Poor dumb buggers, look at 'em. Four beasts of burden."

RACHEL Heaps of skeletons, gold from their teeth.

JESSICA I said, "Mum, the windowpanes are crying."

RACHEL Deaf, blind, incapacitated Heaven.

RUTH   Still can't get past "K" without a headache
                     comin' on.

RACHEL   Kike, yid, hebe.

JESSICA   My nose is better than yours.

                     Brief pause, position change.

RUTH   I'm the one with a curse on my life.

JESSICA   I peed my pants everytime my dad hit me.

RACHEL   I had four, sixteen dollar outfits from Sears'
                     Catalogue.

RUTH   I had callouses on my hands, corns on my toes.

JESSICA   I was out working at eleven.

                     Brief pause. Position change.

JESSICA   He was a brutal, battering son-of-a-bitch.

RUTH   Where could I go? What could I do?

JESSICA   My God, what was the glue between those two?

                     *POLLY enters, taking a position close
                     to RACHEL.*

RUTH   I had the longest, thickest hair. It drove Cam
                     MacMillan crazy.

RACHEL   And then I'd wait for a further heightening. It was
                     promised, after all, by Molly Bloom.

JESSICA   I lived with that man for eight years in absolute
                     trust. Why did he go? When did he go? With
                     whom did he go?

POLLY   I've been looking for dimples like that since I
                     was twelve.

RACHEL   (*to POLLY*)
                She'll rise at dawn
                And it will fall to her
                To wash the semen from the sheets
                And bear the child.

                Brief pause, position change.

JESSICA   He said, "If you learn to type, you don't even
                need Grade Twelve."

RACHEL   I said, "It's your immigrant mentality that makes
                you do that."

RUTH   She said, "You're supposed to learn this when
                you're nine."

POLLY   They said, "We have something to tell you."

JESSICA   I said, "It may be fatal, Gerald, when can you
                come?"

POLLY   We thought they were in love. We thought we
                were secure.

JESSICA   He said, "Let me check my calendar."

                *Brief pause, position change for the
                final lap. JESSICA should now be apart
                from the others.*

JESSICA   I dialed nine-one-one and an ambulance came.

RUTH   Terrible job. Handling it all. Packing it up.

RACHEL   Finding bits of their hair in the brush bristles.

JESSICA   Never again, for me. Fini.

                RACHEL goes back to the crossword.

JESSICA   (*alone, centerstage*) But who will be here to dine?

	Pause. End of the "litany". They change positions.
POLLY	(*exploding*) I tell you, he isn't coming! He probably isn't even on the road!
RACHEL	Stop that! I simply can not stand your damned, inherited histrionics! (*at the crossword*) Oh, for Christ's sake, why do they do this?
JESSICA	What?
RACHEL	These oblique definitions make my blood boil. "Stored fodder." In six. Could be any damned crop that grows in the ground.
RUTH	Wheat?
RACHEL	No, that's —
RUTH	Rye?
JESSICA	Mum, it has to —
RUTH	Oats?
POLLY	Gramma, it's six —
RUTH	Barley?
RACHEL	Barley's six, but it doesn't fit.
RUTH	Alfalfa?
RACHEL	Ruth —
RUTH	(*in frustration*) Oh, for God's sake, try silage!
RACHEL	Silage! That's it. Thank you very much. (*writing it in*) And this one! I swear, I've got creeping Alzheimer's! "Broadway and opera star of the fifties." In five.
POLLY	Pinza.

JESSICA	What?
RACHEL	What did you say?
POLLY	Ezio Pinza.
JESSICA	How do you know that?
POLLY	Martin told me. He took me to see a revival of *South Pacific* in March.
JESSICA	What? What?

JESSICA falls apart, visibly.

JESSICA	While I was ... reading ... at Notre Dame?
POLLY	Yes! Geez, what's the big —
JESSICA	(*falling on POLLY*) Thank you! (*kissing her, wildly*) Oh, thank you, thank you, thank you. Oh, my God, you've saved my soul. (*the doorbell rings*) Oh, God! Oh, Jesus — that's him!
RUTH	(*jumping up, removing her apron*) He's here!
RACHEL	(*removing her apron*) Thank God!
POLLY	(*to the heavens, with her hands in prayer*) Thank you, thank you, thank you. (*reaching out, to JESSICA*) Mama, come with me.
JESSICA	I can't!
POLLY	You have to!
JESSICA	I'm a wreck! Look at me! I can't.
RUTH	Jess MacMillan, mind your manners! Go and greet that boy.

JESSICA and POLLY begin to exit,
then stand together at the specific 'exit'
for a moment. JRSSICA touches
POLLY's arm — a reassuring pat that is
also a slight push away, a letting go.
POLLY exits. Three pin-spots light the
three women left on stage.

RUTH digs down into a pocket to find a
pair of earrings. As she puts them on
RACHEL finds and puts on her shoes.

RUTH and RACHEL then take
positions on either side of the entrance
to the deck. They are "in their heads"
and don't look at each other. They are,
yet again in their late lives, "on the
brink" of something as they wait for
Charles Whitman.

The End.